THE PRIDE OF PARK AVENUE

by

TORIANO PORTER

authorHOUSE®

AuthorHouse™
1663 Liberty Drive, Suite 200
Bloomington, IN 47403
www.authorhouse.com
Phone: 1-800-839-8640

First published by AuthorHouse 11/14/2008

ISBN: 978-1-4389-1347-6 (sc)

Printed in the United States of America
Bloomington, Indiana

This book is printed on acid-free paper.

Dedicated to you, the reader. Thank you for taking the time out of your life to step into my world.

TABLE OF CONTENT

Foreword and introduction   1

Praise for the Pride of Park Avenue   3

SECTION I: LIFE REFLECTIONS   5

Park Avenue Prolouge   9

The Good Die Young   12

The Good Die Young, Part II   16

The Good Die Young, Part III
(for Meko and Jasmine)   20

The City of No Luv   23

The City of No Luv, Part II   38

Shed So Many Tears   45

Shed So Many Tears, Part II   49

Shed So Many Tears, Part III   53

SECTION II: SHORT STORIES,
FLASH FICTION AND MORE   55

The Swinging Gate featuring Rory L. Watkins   57

No Ordinary Day featuring Rory L. Watkins   60

Straddlin' The Fence (Part I)   65

More Colors   73

Straddlin' The Fence (Part II)   76

Five Deep (Me and My Gang)   81

A Place Where Hoop Dreams Dare To Live   86

A Mighty Fine Introduction   94

She's Got It   99

Three Month Fling (You Lousy Son of a Bitch)   105

General Isaiah   108

April's Nobody's Fool   110

Age Ain't Nothing But A Number, Right?   114

With or Without the Ring   117

Background Check   119

The Evening Whirl   120

The Pride of St. Louis   131

SECTION III: GONZO BLOG ENTRIES   141

(My) Definition of Gonzo   143

The Winds of Change   144

Butterflies   146

(I Wonder If I'll Ever See Her) Again   150

Catch Me Now (I'm Fallin')   154

Hanging By a Moment   161

Follow Me   166

SECTION IV: POEMS   173

No Luv   175

Reflections   177

A Boy Named Paul by Rory L. Watkins   182

Dearest Jesus by Rory L. Watkins   183

SECTION V: PREVIEW OF CIRCA 1985,   185

Chapter 1:Adios Park Avenue   187
Chapter 2: Love at First Sight   192
Chapter 3:Hot Summer Nights   194
Chapter 4: A Brand New Day   199
Chapter 5: New Found Friend   204
Chapter 6: Field of Dreams   212
Chapter 7:The JVL Posse   216

ABOUT THE AUTHOR: 221

FOREWORD AND INTRODUCTION

Dr. R.M. Kinder, MFA
Author, *An Absolute Gentleman*

Some years ago, a very personable student in one of my creative writing courses at Central Missouri State University – now UCM - submitted a piece of fiction so vital and engaging that I was stricken with admiration, either for his talent or stricken with disbelief for his audacity to turn in another's as his own.

To prove the authenticity of the work, I asked the student if he could write like that on the spot -say at my computer in my office inside the university's English Department. The work would have to be different from the submitted piece, but still hold the same tone, style and vernacular. Sure, he said, and we set a time.

When he came to my office, he was jovial, amused, obviously pleased at the challenge, and explained that he wasn't at all offended at my doubts of authorship, but was instead complimented.

He sat down to the task, and in moments erased all doubt: His prose was quick, vivid, humorous and poignant. So original it couldn't be imitation and couldn't be imitated.

That young writer was Toriano Porter.

Recently, I've had the pleasure of reading Toriano's first book, The Pride of Park Avenue, a complex, yet remarkable tribute to a community and the individuals that compose it. It's real life; sex, violence, drugs, humor and pathos. The characters and setting are memorable, and the style varied and immediate. He has an ear and heart especially for the spoken word, and captures the poetry of natural speech—a description of his style would pale in comparison to it.

But the strongest trait, even though perhaps it's the most subtle, is the underlying, consistent tone of his work. While he's making us laugh, cry, and/or flinch, his overall view of the community (and one suspects the world) is compassion and optimism. We can't miss that. He's a talented writer, and the book is a good and worthy read.

--R.M. Kinder

PRAISE FOR THE PRIDE OF PARK AVENUE

"When Toriano Porter tells his tales of Park Avenue, he's not referring to the glit and glut of Manhattan's famed boulevard of power and good fortune. Porter's Park Avenue is a concrete cemetery in a war zone in America's Heartland – a desolate street corner pocked by savagery and grit.

Much like a war correspondent, Porter escorts the reader into a world otherwise forbidden and largely unknown by Middle Class Americans. His use of authentic street language, vivid characterization and compelling plots are reminiscent of James Baldwin and Langston Hughes.

But Porter does not leave his readers without hope: for within these pages, one also will find redemption, fueled by a community-in-crisis that simply refuses to be labeled collateral damage.

Porter's work is indeed remarkable – a credible update on today's Street Corner USA – and a welcomed contribution to 21st century American literature." - Rhiannon Ross, American writer and journalist

****

"Okay. Wow. I loved it. I think you are an excellent writer, and you're ability to recount conversations with raw, real talk and slang in a way that flows to the reader is excellent. I can say this; I didn't want it to end. I kept scrolling down at the end to see where the next chapter was.

We all have a story of loss, pain, and betrayal. I know so many adolescents, teens, and adults who would relate to your book.

I have so many kids I see who hate to read or have trouble read-ing -- but would be totally engaged by your stories.

Your book teaches the lessons that I try to help kids to under-stand. I wish your book was used as a text book for high school literature classes.

If I could sum up your stories in a single word: resilience."–Amy Brown Gander, youth counselor, Youth In Need

SECTION I

TRUE LIFE REFLECTIONS

Park Avenue Prologue

The Good Die Young

The Good Die Young, Part II

The Good Die Young, Part III

The City of No Luv

The City of No Luv, Part II

Shed So Many Tears

Shed So Many Tears, Part II

Shed So Many Tears, Part III

…reprinted from the St. Louis Post-Dispatch July 24, 1994…
IN BARREN SOIL, MAKESHIFT CROSSES MULTI-PLY
by Thom Gross of the Post-Dispatch

TEN CRUDE CROSSES fashioned from scrap lumber and cardboard stand on the vacant lot at Park and Louisiana Avenues. Each bears the name of someone killed on the lot or nearby.

The lot has come to symbolize the city's soaring homicide rate and the frustration of residents and police at the inability to stop the bloodshed.

The killing field…is in the heart of what for more than a decade has been one of the city's hottest drug markets.--*Copyright 1994 St. Louis Post-Dispatch Record Number: 9407230437*

Park Avenue Prolouge

My guess is nearly everyone in the city of St. Louis has as much pride in their neighborhood as I have in mine. Although the Southside community in which I was reared - the 3400 block of Park Avenue in the city's Gate District - is a complicated place, it's a place I love and know best.

Over the years, I have experienced Park Ave. in varying degrees. From the sandlot ball-playing days of the 1980's to the dope-slanging, gang-banging, thugged out highs of the '90's, to the weed-selling, ecstasy-popping phase of the new millennium, the eclectic charm of Park Ave., to me, has stood the test of time.

As a collective group of neighbors, we've loved, we've lost, we've prospered, we've struggled and we have always worked hard for what we deemed properly ours. We have made sure our place in the annals of historical neighborhoods in The City wouldn't and couldn't ever be denied.

Victorian-Style homes with freshly manicured grass, privacy fences and plushy-furnished patios dotted the block in my early years. A mixture of red brick single-family homes, two and four family flats and a few apartments lined both sides of Park Avenue from the 3300 block closer to Grand Boulevard down to the 3500 block near Compton Avenue. Several families owned their homes including the Porters, different clans of Elliotts and McKinneys, the Turners, the Watsons, the Mitchells, the Kennedys, the Halls, the Burtons, the Davis' and many others.

Confectionaries like Mr. Joe's and Mr. Henry's candy store provided youthful entertainment with snacks and video games. Wood's Liquor Store provided the proverbial grown folks action and Watson's Funeral Home was a gathering place to remember those gone on to a better place. As time went on, Big Business drove away small business and property owners and a few renters. Still, those who stayed made their way.

Parents, grandparents, relatives, in-laws, cousins, aunts, uncles, sisters and brothers all contributed in some form to the make-up of the community. We may have not been the most politically active or the most benevolent, but we looked out for our own and we rarely backed down for what we believed in.

Growing up as kids we dealt with the elements of drugs, crime and violence that seemingly infiltrated urban neighborhoods throughout the country. We were oblivious to it all, although the negative vibes of the hood would gradually seep into our bloodstream.

Before the maturation process, we shared our adolescent youth revolving with the seasons. In the summer it was, of course, baseball at Terry Park and softball at Wyman Elementary School. In the fall, there were pick-up basketball games at Terry Park, Wyman, Gallaudet School for the Blind or the neighboring Buder Park. The winter months didn't deter our athletic aspirations for it was not a thing to line up and play a snow-filled Turkey Bowl sandlot football game. In the spring, we'd trade off between kill-a-man football, three-on-three basketball or slow pitch softball with the young ladies of the neighborhood.

As my generation got older, a majority soured on school and hit the bricks. The violent culture of the St. Louis streets seemed to overtake attending high school regularly, playing ball or being law-abiding citizens. The late 1980's and early 1990's were a definite struggle within my peer group. Our hood became known as one of the city's hottest drug markets. With it came the requisite bloodshed.

In the new millennium, Saint Louis University expanded; purchasing property and homes in an attempt to build whatever it is that universities build when they displaced life-long citizens of a particular locale. Cardinal Glennon Children's Hospital best-laid plans and private investors also slowly but surely weeded out most of the property owners left and drove out most of the nonsense that had been associated with the block the last three decades or so. Even still, the 3300 block of Vista Street, our kindred neighbors one block over to the north, provided temporary reprieve for guys to set up shop and continue the hood's legacy.

Park Ave. is what it is; what it always has been and what it will continue to be; home. Growing up there, we all had a chance, we all had a choice. It was a residential place, not a government-subsidized dwelling or a gang infested housing project. Park Ave. was a community that once thrived with commerce, love and a sense of worth.

Although the neighborhood produced some of the Southside's more ambitious gang-bangers, money stacking dope-slangers, cold-blooded killers, ruthless car-jackers and hardened thugs, it also has produced talented professional athletes, award-winning movie and music producers, savvy business-minded barber and beauty shop owners, dedicated city firefighters and other city personnel, successful real estate investors and countless other respectable, tax-paying nine-to-fivers.

Speaking as a whole, we are a proud flock. Damn sure proud to be where we're from. We carry that pride with a swagger wherever we go. We wear our neighborhood affiliation like a badge of honor. As the powers that be take what we once called ours, we will always be what we are. We are Park Avenue and we are Park Avenue proud.

...reprinted from the St. Louis Post-Dispatch June 23, 1990...
VIOLENT DEATHS: Delancy M. Davis, *22, of the 3400 block of Park Avenue, died early Friday after being shot on the street corner Thursday night in the 3400 block of Park.* **Davis** *was shot at 9:45 p.m. Thursday and died at 1:42 a.m. Friday at St. Louis University Hospital. Homicide Capt. Robert Baumann said detectives were looking for a man who ran from the scene after firing five or six shots at* **Davis**. *The motive for the shooting was undetermined. --Copyright 1990 St. Louis Post-Dispatch*

THE GOOD DIE YOUNG

The vacant lot at Park and Louisiana Avenues in South St. Louis is a notorious hot spot in The City. The appropriately titled 'Killing Field' has held that crime-riddled distinction for the better part of the last three decades. A few of my close friends have lost their life on that lot or nearby in the 3400 block of Park Avenue

For as long as I can remember The Lot has always been just that -- The Lot -- a place to hang out, play ball, drink brew and pig out on barbeque. It was sort of the 3400 block's urban hangout suite--complete with balding, brownish grass, un-recycled glass and a plethora of debris and trash.

The City, up until being purchased by private investors, was responsible for its upkeep, but you know how that went--one month they'd clean it, the next month they'd ignore it.

For me, The Lot was very much apart of my upbringing — from playing baseball and football to foot racing and having brick fights. The Lot was what symbolized The Block; fun-loving, nurturing and caring to outright cruel and unusual punishment.

The first person close to me to die near the unpopulated parcel of land was my older brother's best friend, Delancy M. Davis.

Delancy was a cool dude. Medium in height, Delancy was a peculiar mix of street soldier and sports star. Despite being an unusual combination of bow-legged and pigeon-toed, he was the fastest, most athletic cat in the neighborhood. He had a burn scar on his lip, a constant reminder of sticking his tongue in an electrical outlet at the Davis' home as a mischievous tot.

Delancy was also the first person from our neighborhood peer group to play organized baseball. I sort of dug that.

Honestly, he was a role model to me. I remember when he used to walk through The Block wearing his brown and gold A.G. Edwards baseball uniform, circa 1982.

"Main (Delancy's nickname)," I said to him on one of those hot, early 80's summer afternoons, "who you play for?"

Main, six years my senior, was callous in his response.

"Don't worry about lil' runt, you can't play."

"Naw, serious man," I countered, "who do you play for."

"Why man?" he shot back.

"'Cause I wanna play."

"You ain't old enough, you lil' runt?"

I was stoked. In fact, that day I was determined I was going to play summer ball for A.G. Edwards some day and show Main I could handle mines on the baseball field. Although I never played for A.G. Edwards, the competitive fire was lit.

Back then, we used to play baseball daily during the summer on The Lot. Every time I wanted to be on Delancy's team because he was the oldest and always picked the best team. He never picked me, though.

As Delancy got older, his passion for the game quivered. Slowly his athletic skills faded as his street savvy soared. By the time he was sixteen, he was doing time at The City's Juvenile Detention Center on Vandeventer Avenue.

One day, after he had gotten out of Juvey, my older brother and I were jiving with Delancy about getting beaten up while he was locked down. Come to find out later, Delancy actually put a whooping on the dude, but you know how it goes when you are ten and twelve -- as me and my brother were at the time -- you just want a good laugh. By the time Delancy got finish mopping up the concrete with us, he was the one with the last laugh

"The fag pop and the runt," Delancy barked at us after the one-sided ruckus. "Ya'll some suckas."

Delancy also had the distinction of tagging my older brother with the coolest nickname known to man: Bean Pole. We were all hanging out in The Hood one day, circa 1987, when Delancy hit my brother, birth name Antoine, with one of Delancy's famous barbs.

"Ya'll ever seen that episode of Good Times when Thelma and JJ get into it," Delancy asked a few of the hoodfellas.

My brother, a tall, rangy youngster, did remind some of JJ Evans in stature - tall and toothpick thin. He really favored JJ Evans when he donned a turtleneck sweater, as he happened to have on the day Delancy branded him with the moniker.

"'Member?" Delancy continued, "when she was like 'forget you, Bean Pole!'". "Don't that nigga look like JJ Evans in that mother-fuckin' turtleneck? Nigga, that's yo' name from now on. We gon' call this nigga Bean Pole, ya'll!"

Three years later my brother and Delancy were running mates, two of the most respected young hustlers in South St. Louis.

Early in the summer of 1990 things were scorching in The City. I'm not just talking about those hot and humid days either. The City was blazing with urban warfare as different factions of gangs, sets and neighborhoods claimed stake to their illusionary territory.

In the process lives were lost, families were displaced, and some, like me, lost heroes. Delancy was one of those heroes.

I had just gotten back from a summer league baseball game in University City when my mother delivered the news. We had moved from Park Avenue years before, so I was standing on the front porch steps of the three-bedroom townhouse we lived in on James Cool Papa Bell Street in North St. Louis. I couldn't do anything after I learned of Delancy's plight but damn the air and head to the Southside with my mother.

By the time I got to The Block, Park Avenue was hopping mad. Information gathering police officers, distraught family members, revenge seeking hoodfellas and curious by-standers alike, all peppered the street.

"What happened?" I asked a cousin as I surveyed the scene.

My cousin, who was just six months older than me, was running the streets with Main and my brother like most of the guys from The Block. I was still stunned when he gave me the scoop.

"Some fool blasted on Main," he said, casually displaying the chrome plated .32 automatic he had stashed in his hip. "They working on him right now up at Saint Louis U."

My thoughts immediately turned toward my brother. Where was he? Where is he? Did he get shot too? After all, they were ace boon coons at that time.

"Carlyle, where Bean Pole at?"

"He's up at the hospital right now."

"Is he alright?"

"Yeah, Mo. He was at the mall when the shit went down, but mugs know who did it."

"Yeah?"

"Yeah," Carlyle said, again brandishing the pistol.

The circumstances behind Delancy's death have never been very important to me. The fact that he was killed so prematurely has never sat right with me and I guess this is my way of coming to grips with that. This is my shout out to the life in which he lived, per se.

Delancy was a hero to me because he was the first person from The Block to show me there was more to the world than just the two-block radius of the 'hood. He was somebody I figured could have been anything in the world he wanted to be. Delancy provided so many precious memories. I'll always treasure those memories of seeing him in his AG Edwards baseball uniform. I'll never treasure the sight of seeing him laid to rest at Watson's Funeral Home. Never. Much love to the Davis family and know that we all still miss you, Main.

...reprinted from the St. Louis Post-Dispatch April 25, 1993...
2 KILLED IN CITY IN SHOOTINGS NO ARRESTS, SUSPECTS IN EITHER SLAYING
by Kim Bell of the Post-Dispatch Staff

A teen-ager who had been robbed went out onto the streets of St. Louis to find the people who robbed him, police say. Early Saturday, he was found in a vacant lot, fatally shot in the head.

About 1 a.m. Saturday, **Damon Hamilton**, 18, was found lying in a vacant lot at 3401 Park Avenue, in the Lafayette Towne neighborhood, police said. **Hamilton** was pronounced dead on arrival at St. Louis University Hospital.--*Copyright 1993 St. Louis Post-Dispatch*

THE GOOD DIE YOUNG, PART II

"Oh, you ain't heard? They found Lil' Damon dead on The Lot about a week ago."

Those were the words spoken to me by my Aunt Phyllis as she delivered the awful news in response to my inquiry concerning the whereabouts of my "cousin", Damon Hamilton, circa April 1993.

Lil' Damon was the second eldest son of my mother's good friend, Diane Hamilton. Although they were not actually blood relatives, Diane and my mother called themselves sisters, thus leaving me and my siblings to refer to Diane's four piece—which also included Vernell, August and Jab—as cousins.

I had known Lil' Damon since kindergarten—we were actually in the same ABC, 123 learning class. Always small in stature, Lil' Damon, as well as the eldest son Vernell, had a big heart. I remember being semi-lost that first day of kindergarten, looking for a familiar face to shun the pain of my mother leaving me at bay.

"Wants some candy," Lil' Damon offered that first day of school. "My mama told me to make sure I gave you some of my candy if I saw you at school."

The episode created a bond between me and Lil' Damon that would last for years. Even though we wound up on two distinct paths in life—Lil' Damon dropped out of Parkway West High while I graduated from Eureka High and went on to college—we always remained loyal to our friendship and trust in one another.

I was home freshman year for spring break from Central Missouri State University in Warrensburg, Missouri in late March, 1993 when I ran into Lil' Damon. The barely five-foot, five inch, 140 pound pretty boy thug had just completed an extended stint at the Medium Security Lockup in North St. Louis. I was standing on my grandmother's porch in the 3400 block of Park Avenue when I noticed him one block up, fraternizing with Christy, a distant cousin of mine. Being that Damon and I weren't actual blood relatives and Christy was a cousin through marriage, it was all good for those two to date. I still chided him about it, though.

"Hey, nigga," I said in a mock machismo tone. "What'chu doing wit' yo' hands all over my lil' cousin?"

"Tory?" Lil' Damon said, focusing in on my impromptu visit up the Park Avenue street I had called home for most of my life. "Nigga, what'chu doing here? I thought you was 'spose to be at school."

"I'm here on Spring Break. What's up with you?" I said, noticing Lil' Damon was a bit off-kilter.

"Nothing, man, just got back out here for real," he replied, his now apparent stupor more visible by the slur, "trying to make some shit happen."

I hadn't seen much of Lil' Damon since leaving for college some seven months prior, but it was obvious he was high on something. I instinctively surmised heroin. It was the wayward youths' of South St. Louis drug of choice back then. It didn't matter to me, though, I was just happy he was out of the Medium Security lock-up on the edge of North St. Louis.

"Back on these corners, huh?" I deadpanned, trying to find an angle to motivate.

"Gotta get that dough, T, you know how that go?"

I understood the concept of feeling trapped. I understood the allure of the street corner mentality.

I understood Lil' Damon. I understood his situation and I understood his plight. I couldn't do much for his addiction to the action of the streets, but I offered all I could at the time.

"Dawg, check this out," I said, as I wrapped up my hustle stagnating greeting, "I'm going back to Warrensburg in two days and I want you to go back with me."

"Warrensburg?" Lil' Damon scoffed. "Where the hell is Warrensburg?"

"Up by Kansas City," I chimed, proud to know more about Missouri than just The Block

"Ain't nothin' but a four hour train ride."

"What's the name of your school, again" he hazily asked, as if really interested.

"Central Missouri State."

"Central Missouri State? Kansas City, huh?"

"Naw, man, it's in Warrensburg…about 45 minutes from Kansas City."

"What you do up there, you play ball?"

"Football, nigga. You'ont know?"

"Football, huh? I always knew you was gon' do some shit like that. You goin' pro, nigga?"

"Damn right, I'm going pro. But, I gotta get on the field first"

"You'ont start?"

"Hell, naw. Them motherfuckas red-shirted me this year. But it's all good. I'ma start next year."

"What position, wide receiver?"

"Nope. Free safety."

"Free safety? Nigga, you can't hit."

"Man, okay! You better ask somebody."

After that exchange, I could sense Lil' Damon may have wanted to take me up on the offer, but he remained uncommitted to the trip.

"Let me get out here and see what I can make happen," he said before departing back into his lovenest/hustle mode. "When you say you leaving?"

"Sunday morning. Train leaves at 7:30 in the morning, but if you want to you can take the afternoon train. It leaves at 3:30."

"Hey look, T, I'ma come holla at'chu before you go and let you know what's up. Where you gon' be, at yo' grandmama's house?"

"Yep. Make sure you get at me though, man. The shit's fun. It's peaceful and it'll give you a chance to get back from all this shit here-- I ain't gon' even tell you about the girls. College girls? College girls the biggest freaks, dawg."

"Word?"

"Word, nigga, you gotta come."

"Bet. I'm coming. I'ma holla at'chu before you leave though aw'ight?"

"Aw'ight, cool."

I returned to school from spring break without Lil' Damon. I had seen him on The Block a few hours after our initial conversation, but that was the last I saw of him before I headed back. I left specific instructions for my Aunt Phyllis, who had dropped me off at the Amtrak Station in Downtown St. Louis.

"If you see Lil' Damon, make sure you give him my number," I barked before unloading.

Nearly a month had passed and I hadn't heard from either Lil' Damon nor my aunt. I placed a phone call to my Grandma's house in hopes of my aunt catching Lil' Damon loitering about on The Block. A few party-goers at CMSU were having a kick-ass party the weekend before final exams and I wanted Lil' Damon to make due on his plans to visit.

I reached my Aunt that April day and that's when she gave me the low-down on Lil' Damon's untimely passing. I was hard-pressed for questions and my aunt was just as pressed for answers.

She didn't know much about the circumstances. All she could tell me was they found him dead on The Lot—shot in the head. I never got a chance to see him laid to rest. In some ways, I'm sort of thankful for that. I'll always have those memories of kindergarten and the street corner pep talk I spilled before his death, instead of seeing him in that pine box. We miss you Lil' Damon and thank you for sharing those wonderful--but all to brief--eighteen years with us.

...reprinted from the St. Louis Post-Dispatch January 14, 1994...
DISTURBANCE FOLLOWS DRUG-RAID KILLING; CITY POLICE ARREST 13 AS FAMILY OF TEEN SHOT BY OFFICER GATHERS NEAR APARTMENT
By Tim O'Neil and Bill Bryan of the Post-Dispatch

Police arrested 13 men Thursday afternoon at an angry gathering outside an apartment where a police officer fatally shot a young man during a drug raid.

Officer Michael O'Hare shot **DeAndreis McKinney** once in the head Wednesday at a four-family flat in the 3400 block of Park Avenue, investigators said. Police said they found a derringer with one round in **McKinney**'s hand.

Homicide supervisors said their initial investigation shows that O'Hare, 29, acted properly.—*Copyright 1994 St. Louis Post-Dispatch*

THE GOOD DIE YOUNG, PART III
(FOR MEKO AND JASMINE)

My daily reading habits had weaned a bit the early part of spring semester 1994 when I made the first of what was supposed to be a weekly retreat to Ward Edward's Library on the campus of Central Missouri State University in Warrensburg. The previous semester I had made the every seventh day cross-campus jaunt to catch up on what was happening in my hometown of St. Louis, Missouri.

The trek usually ended by me reading the previous week's issues of the *St. Louis Post-Dispatch*, which Ward Edwards carried, albeit three days after the *Post* went to press.

Anyway, on this particular January evening I ran across an article in the Metro section that would send debilitating shockwaves down the depths of my spine. My good friend from the neighborhood in which I was reared, DeAndreis "Meko" McKinney, had been shot and killed—by an officer with the STLPD no less.

The article said, according to police, Meko had attempted to flee police during a drug raid on a unit in a four-family flat in the 3400 block of Park Avenue. The article read the police said Meko pointed a gun at the firing officer as Meko fled. The officer then proceeded to shoot Meko in the head.

In all fairness, I wasn't there, so speculation on my part would be insidious. I don't want to open old wounds--not only for the family's sake, but the officers' sake as well.

It gnaws at me though—"it" being the unnerving circumstances behind Meko's death. The article read, again, according to police Meko pointed a derringer with one round at the officer, prompting the justified shooting issued after the incident. St. Louis was in a full-fledged drug/gun/gang craze in the early parts of 1994. The City had just set its' infamous record of murders in 1993, so gunplay was a semi-normal way of life for ghetto soldiers confined to the walls of inner-city warfare.

Parts of Park Avenue were known drug hot-spots throughout the Third Police District in the nineties. That being said, its hard to believe that anybody—including Meko--dabbling in a life of crime would have in their possession—in a known drug spot during urban warfare at its' height—a one shot derringer. Either way, much to the chagrin of family and friends, the shooting remained justified.

When I read the article I remembered feeling angered, upset, disappointed and heartbroken. I mean, Meko was my homie, you know? Good people from a good family. Like many inner-city youths, he was faced with choices and he made the most of those choices. Those choices--good, bad or indifferent--can never take the place of who he was; a caring father, a loyal son, a protective brother, a trustworthy cousin, a dependable nephew, a dedicated friend.

Just six months prior to his death I had a domestic dispute involving a girlfriend and an ex. The ex had paid an unwarranted visit to my Grandma's house while I was entertaining the new girlfriend. It was the summer before my sophomore year of college, so I was having a ball playing the field.

The ex, accompanied by her mother and her mother's boyfriend, became a bit unruly when my Grandma asked the ex to leave the premises. The confrontation, verbal in nature only, had spilled onto the front porch of my Grandma's house, prompting an immediate disruption to the neighborhood's normal flow of summer activity.

"T.P.," a serious looking Meko menacingly said. He had walked upon the situation just as the ex's mother and step-father pitch their two cents into the argument. "Errrthang cool?"

"Yeah," I responded casually, all the while trying to keep the ex from pummeling the new chick, "everything cool, cuzz." Meko nodded and headed back down Park Ave to tend his business, leaving me and my Grandma to horde off the bum's rush from the ex and her temporary goons (which, by the way, ended peacefully).

Meko, we miss you, you big Sloppy Dog. I'll never forget you had that "bounty" out on me and Big Emmett Staples when we (Eureka High) played Roosevelt High in football back in 1990. You kept trying to sneak me after the whistle, but I could hear your big ass footsteps. See you when I see you Big Homie. Stay Solid. Stay Gold. RIP to your daughter Jasmine. You guys are re-united baby boy.

...reprinted from the St. Louis Post-Dispatch September 30, 1993...

EX-HIGH SCHOOL FOOTBALL STAR SHOT DEAD WALKING NEAR HOME

A college student who was a former all-district football player was shot and killed Wednesday while he walked with relatives in the 6000 block of Garesche Avenue in the Walnut Park area, police said.

The victim, **Wesley Drummond**, 20, had shotgun wounds to the chest, shoulders and hand. He was taken to Barnes Hospital, where he later died. **Drummond** was a student at Central Missouri State University in Warrensburg, authorities said.

He was an all-district football player at Parkway Central High School in 1990.-- *Copyright 1993 St. Louis Post-Dispatch*

THE CITY OF NO LUV

(inspired by and written for Wesley Maurice "Milk" Drummond)

Every time I saw Rod Smith catch a touchdown pass for the Denver Broncos during his 13-year career in the NFL, I got teary eyed. Not because I'm a fan, (although I am a **huge** Rod Smith fan) or because he overcame serious knee injuries to become one of the all-time premier pass receivers in the NFL. I got moist eyes because of what Rod Smith represented to me; toughness, desire, athletic ability and heart.

On background, Smith signed with Denver as an undrafted free agent out of Missouri Southern prior to the 1994 season, and went on to amass 849 career receptions, 11,389 receiving yards and 68 touchdowns in 183 games with the Broncos.

A three-time Pro Bowl selection, Smith ranks seventh in career games played with the Broncos and holds the NFL career record for receptions, receiving yards and touchdown catches by an undrafted player.

At the time of his retirement, the 6-foot, 190-pounder ranked 12th on the NFL's career receptions list, and his nine-year streak of catching at least 70 passes each season from 1997 through 2005 ties for the second longest in league history.

Smith spent his rookie season on the Broncos practice squad but became an integral member of two Super Bowl champions and seven Denver playoff squads. He set team records with 49 total post-season receptions, 860 receiving yards and six playoff touchdowns. In Denver's Super Bowl XXXIII win over Atlanta, Smith had 152 receiving yards -- tied for fifth-best in Super Bowl history.

I have never met Rod Smith in person although I had an opportunity to see him play twice in college. Well, actually I got a chance to see him play one full game and one quarter of another one.

Let me explain. The first time I saw Rod Smith play, I was a redshirt freshman football player at Central Missouri State University in Warrensburg in the fall of 1992. We were playing host to the Missouri Southern Lions. We came into the contest sporting a 3-1 record and Mo. Southern was undefeated at 4-0, so it was a pretty big early season conference game.

To tell you the truth, most MIAA (Mid-America Intercollegiate Athletic Association) Conference games were big games considering you had to play against the likes of perennial Division II powers Pittsburg State, Missouri Western, Emporia State, Northeast Missouri State (now Truman) Washburn (yes, Washburn was a torn in Central Mo's side) and of course, Mo Southern. Northwest Missouri State had not yet become the class of the MIAA. Any of those teams could claim potential pro ball players and various D-II All-Americans amongst their roster.

Missouri Southern came into the game explosive on offense and athletic on defense. We were the exact opposite; dominating on defense and athletic on offense. (In this tense, athletic refers to good athletes on their respective sides of the ball, but as a unit, not very proficient).

The Lions boasted an array of talented performers on offense, including lefty quarterback Matt Cook, a tall and rangy Rod Smith, a bruising tailback in Karl Evans and a stout offensive line.

On the other hand, Central Mo. countered with a Dirty Red defense that was nationally ranked #1, 2, or 3 in total yards allowed per game, total points allowed per game and turnover margin. Not bragging, but I was a pretty heralded D-II recruit but I never stepped on the field that year because we had 14 pretty good defensive backs and ten of them got ample playing time. Hell, I couldn't even crack the special teams unit that season.

Out of four defensive back positions, we had four dope starters, four solid backups and two more ball-hawks who played both the safety and cornerback positions. One of those ball-hawks was a sophomore from Parkway Central High named Wesley Maurice

Drummond. We called him Milk because he never drank alcohol, didn't use drugs and hardly lifted weights. Hell, he didn't even drink milk, but he was so naturally cut and strong the name just fit.

When I first met Milk the summer prior to that season, we didn't quite hit it off too well. He was from the Walnut Park (North Side) area of The City and I was off The Block in South Saint Louis. His particular set was a blood set and my preference was to the guys in blue (and I'm not talking about the STLPD).

After that intensely hot summer camp of two-a-day practices, we bonded in a teammate sort of way. It was no longer a personal beef between us being from opposite ends of the gangbang spectrum, but love and respect that comes from going through football's version of a military boot camp.

Like I was saying, Mo. Southern had a deadly one-two punch at quarterback and receiver. Fortunately, Cook, the quarterback, had been injured the week before and was ruled out for the game against us. So what does Mo Southern do? Yep. They moved Rod Smith to quarterback for the game. Thanks to Milk, we would never see him take a snap from underneath center.

After winning the coin toss we received possession of the football first. Promptly, the offense stalled and we were force to punt.

All week, we had prepared for Rod Smith to return punts. He was very good at it and we prepared accordingly. Milk, who was a back-up at both cornerback and safety that game, was geeked. He knew he wasn't going to be on the field to start the game on defense, but he felt he could set the tone for the defense with a big hit on Rod Smith during punt coverage.

Things started moving slowly for me on the sidelines during that first punt. Although I couldn't play in the game, I was dressed out in our black silky-looking pants, Cardinal red jersey, red and white pro-style socks and a pair of white high-top cleats - complete with crisp, white wrist bands and a fresh pretty boy towel draped from the pants of my uniform. A "C" encrusted red helmet with black stripes shielded my face from joke-laden spectators.

I was watching Milk - taking mental reps as the coaches like to say - because he was the 'gunner' on the punt coverage team, and I hoped I could do that job later on in the season if the coaches decided I was ready to contribute. His job was to 'gun' down the man with the football. In this case it was the All-America Rod Smith

As the ball floated off Denny Cox's - our punter - foot, Milk shook the man responsible for blocking him and was on a streamline bee right at Rod Smith, who stood some forty yards from the line of scrimmage waiting anxiously to return the punt for what he hoped would be another one of his spectacular plays.

Gauging the punt, first I saw Milk glance at Rod Smith. Almost on cue, Rod Smith looked at Milk and in a cruel twist of fate, sized him up for the juke move he had in store, then refocused back on the hanging punt. While this was going on, I looked at them both, then refocused on the ball, as well. Out the corner of my eye, I could see Milky zero in on his prey as the ball descended towards Rod Smith's oversized mitts.

In a blur, I, along with the 8,000 or so people in the stands, heard a thud, a pop and a scream. Within seconds, Milk was hot-stepping and celebrating, as Rod Smith lay in a sprawling heap--yellow flags from the referees abounded the sculptured green grass of Vernon Kennedy Field.

"Trainer! Trainer," one of the Mo. Southern Lions yelled out as their teammate summed up his plight in a painstaking "aaagggghhhh shit."

While the Mo. Southern trainers attended to their fallen stud, Milk was being chastised by our defensive back coach, Mark Hulet, who was being chewed out by our head coach Terry Noland.

"Mark, we can't afford 15-yard penalties," Coach Noland said to Coach Hulet, "get that straightened out would 'ya!"

"O.K. Coach," Coach Hulet politicked, "Wes...."

By that time Milky was amped. Not only had he blown out Rod Smith's knee, he was also penalized fifteen yards for unnecessary roughness; hitting the punt return man before he was allowed to catch the ball. What's crazy is Milk thought he had timed the hit perfectly.

"Man, what?" Milk sniped to Coach Hulet, still in an oversized zone, "what?"

"Time that hit the next time," Coach Hulet said emphatically. "Ease up and time that hit."

During the brief silence that followed Milk's hit, we could hear the moaning and grumbling on the Lions' sidelines. They seemed to think we had a bounty out on Rod Smith but actually all we had was an overly-hyped 'gunner' with bad timing. In fact on the very next punt, Milk did the exact same thing to Rod Smith's replacement, smashing him before he caught the punt, again drawing a 15-yard penalty.

"Coach Hulet," Coach Noland screamed as he ran a forty-yard sprint from the offensive side of the sideline to the defensive side, "get Wes' ass out of there."

Coach Hulet was not defiant about it at all. "It's done Coach, it's done."

For a brief second I was hoping they would put me in the game, but I knew that would never happen without me practicing with the punt coverage team first. I snapped back to reality, walked up to Milk and said "damn, dirty what the f*** is wrong with you."

"Get the hell outta my face Crab ass rookie," Milky exclaimed, "get on the field first before you start popping off at the mouth you gotdamn scrub."

I knew Milk was heated so I pardoned the eruption. Still I couldn't help but feel his frustration. He just wanted to hit somebody. Anybody.

"Calm down, dawg, calm down," I said, "it's the first damn quarter and you got 30 yards worth of penalties."

We went on to win that game, (we finished 6-4 that year) Rod Smith missed the rest of that season with a torn ACL and me and Milk went on to solidify our friendship. "You aw'ight with me Crab ass nigga," Milk would say later on, "you aw'ight with me."

In November, following the '92 season, my teammate and friend Leon Moody and I needed a ride home from Warrensburg to Saint Louis for Thanksgiving break. Since we only socialized with other football players at that time and the Amtrak train was already booked full, our choices for a ride quickly dwindled. In a pinch, Milk came through. Only one catch, though. We had to mob with his Blood homies from Walnut Park who came up to The 'Burg to kick it at a party CMSU hosted before the break.

"Hey, Blood," Milk said to one of his comrades the day he introduced us, "these niggas 'pose to be some Crabs."

"Aw yeah?" his partner countered.

"Yeah," Milk said.

"From where, Blood?"

"Shit, I'on know," Milk chided, "where you niggas from again."

Moody chunked up his North County Hathaway South hood, while I chunked up The Block.

"These niggas claiming hoods mugs ain't never even heard of," Milk jokingly said to his friend. He got serious then. "They aw'ight with me, though, dirty," he said, "these young niggas got some heart."

Milk had become an integral part of me and Moody's lives even though we were on the opposite sides of the gangbang fence. Although Saint Louis was in the middle of a record number murder rate in July of 1993 Moody and I had grown even closer to Milk. That's why I froze up when Moody called me with the news Milk might not play ball for Central in the fall of '93.

"Cuzz," Moody said after I retrieved the phone from my Grandma. "Milk got popped last night."

"What?" I screamed in disbelief. "By who, cuzz?"

"From what I'm hearing," Moody surmised "it was supposed to be a couple of them cats he hangs out with, but I'on know, cuzz."

"Was it them cats we rode home with?" I asked dumbfounded.

"I'on know," Moody said, "but I think it happened over on the North by where them niggas be, but I'on know…they saying he might not be able to play ball this year. Once I find out more I'ma come and swoop you up, cuzz."

Milk used to always wear this fire engine red St. Louis Cardinals baseball jacket with 52euce Mob stitched on the sleeve and No Luv embroidered on the front. I never really fully understood what that meant until Moody called me with the unconfirmed word of Milk's plight. *His own homies, I thought? No wonder he calls this mutha the City of No Luv.*

Moody did come down to The City that July night to picked me up and give me the word on Milk's situation. Seemed details were sketchy--no one knew who the perpetrators actually were and no one we knew could figure out why Milk had gotten shot. All we knew was Milk was laid up in the hospital, expected to live, but unable to play football for the Mules that upcoming '93 season.

Neither Moody nor I got a chance to see Milk until we returned to school that fall, but we never asked him about what happened. We were just happy he was still alive and enjoying life.

A lot had personally changed for me when I enrolled for the fall '93 semester. I had blown the scholarship awarded to me by Coach Noland following my senior year at Eureka High. That red-shirt year affected my grades, as well as my off field behavior. The tomfoolery caught up with me my second year at Central: I was ineligible to play.

So while my red-shirt brethren and fellow scout team members advance from red-shirts to starters (WR's Moody and Sean McIntyre and DB Marlon Johnson among them) in one year, I was stuck in the bleachers, cheering on the Fighting Mules with the rest of the student body.

My only solace was Milk. The injuries from that past summer's shooting had left his hands and wrists a tangled mess so he couldn't play either. We both just stood in the stands and critiqued every missed tackle, dropped ball, bad call (coaches' and referees') and the like.

Well, that was our routine for the first two homes games prior to Missouri Southern and Rod Smith's return to Vernon Kennedy Stadium that season.

The Mules had only played one away game at that point of the season. Milk and I spent that particular afternoon listening to the game on the CMSU radio network, smoking blunts, drinking 40 Ounce brews and bitching about the DB's not making enough plays—even though one of Milk's roommates and best friends, Wayne Carter, and my good friend Marlon Johnson were the starting corners and my mentor Tom Jackson and pro prospect Creston Austin were the starting safeties.

The 1993 Mo. Southern game was different than the one the season before. The '93 game was an afternoon tilt and it was cold, wet and windy. Rod Smith was mad. He was motivated. And he was on a mission.

Milk couldn't take it. Hell, I couldn't even take sitting in the bleachers. We both wanted to be out there. We couldn't, so we did the next best thing. We asked the DB coach, Coach Hulet, if we could stand on the sidelines for the game against Mo. Southern.

"Stand over there and stay outta the way and don't be talking trash to those guys," was all Coach Hulet said. "Remember last year don't you, Wes?"

I stand before this: to this day I say Rod Smith made it to the NFL based on his game against the Mules that late September afternoon. I don't know how many catches he had, but I know he had three touchdown receptions on the Mules that day.

The first one was a pretty left-handed loft from Matt Cook, the QB who sat out the game against the Mules the year before. It covered at least 65 yards—all I can remember is Rod Smith escaping Wayne's Cover 2 jam at the line and Smith subsequently blowing by T.J. (Tom Jackson) at safety.

"Man, what the fuck?" Milk screamed, adjusting the straps on the black hand-wrap like cast he wore on his left mitt. "How they just gon' let that nigga run by them like that, T.P.? Huh! What's that shit?"

The second Rod Smith touchdown came in similar fashion as the first. Somehow Smith escaped our cornerback's jam at the line of scrimmage and streaked toward Vernon Kennedy's south end-zone. This time, the safety, Creston Austin, slipped and fell on the wet surface. Keep in mind, a Cleveland Browns' scout had told Coach Noland and his staff Creston had the best footwork of any college defensive back in the country. Nevertheless, Creston slipped and Rod Smith ended up with another 60-yard plus TD reception from Cook.

"T.P., man that's bullshit," Milk screamed at Creston's plight. "We suppose to be out there, Blood, we suppose to be out there."

The third touchdown was what would become classic Rod Smith. I mean, the two bombs were impressive as hell, but it was his leaping, sprawling catch over Marlon in the north end-zone that solidified Rod Smith's standing in my eyes as the best wide receiver I ever saw play in person. It was a simple fade to the corner of the end-zone-- my boy Marlon, who would become a four-time All-MIAA performer--was draped all over Rod Smith and Smith still caught the ball. Classic.

"Ain't much MJ could have done about that," I said to Milk after Milk's initial response of Smith's third TD. "He was all on that nigga and that motherfu**a still caught the damn ball. That nigga going to the league, cuzz."

We lost the game that year. Mo. Southern had just too many weapons for our Dirty Red Defense, which was still one of the top units in all of Division-II football. Too much Rod Smith to be exact.

After the game, we accompanied the team into the locker room. After hearing Coach Noland's teary-eyed, post-game speech, Milk and I quietly pointed out all the mistakes the defense made. We both were extremely critical of our defensive back brethren, but what could we do about it besides getting back on the field the next year. Ping, as Wayne was affectionately known, didn't want to hear it. M.J. sure as hell didn't want to hear it. T.J. and Creston? We just let them stew in their post-game misery. They both were excellent safeties who just happened to run into a buzz-saw type wide receiver with a grudge.

Milk wanted to talk to Rod Smith after the game. He wanted to apologize. He wanted to talk shit to Smith—sort of congratulate Smith on his game. He wanted to let Smith know there was no bounty the year before. He even wanted to tell Smith about his shooting injuries.

Eventually, Milk simply said "fuck it, that nigga know I ain't have no bounty out on him. I ain't gotta apologize. Let's go get high while these bum ass niggas get dressed…them niggas let that boy score three touchdowns on them T.P. Three! That's bullshit!"

Milk and Ping lived with another Mules' football player, Big Mo (Maurice Zanders) at The Estes Apartments, once a thriving Warrensburg hotel that would later be converted into cheap rental units. The run down, semi-condemned mini high-rise was our little private oasis. Moody and Sean Mac were roommates who lived down the hall from Big Mo, Ping and Milk. Our former running back, Henry Caldwell, who had a tryout with the San Diego Chargers after his eligibility was up, lived in The Estes, too. He had a couple of fellow

Floridians living with him—cousins Cecil and Troy. I had moved out of the dorms at the beginning of the semester into the living room of a pair of female friends from Hannibal, Missouri—Marcia and Markita.

I had met them freshmen year in the dorms and they were mad cool. I didn't want to live in the dorm my second year but Moody and Sean Mac, who were suppose to be my roommates, had moved a defensive end from South Carolina named Willis Moye in right after two-a-days. I didn't return to Warrensburg until school started that fall so they thought I wasn't coming back. But I did and it was too late. Willis had moved in.

Anyway, The Estes was a hop, skip and jump from the locker room. Milk and I were talking about the game on the walk towards The Estes, when I told him about my situation.

"So, you saying your lil' broad finna come drop your son off and ya'll 'bout to get on the train and go back to St. Louis," Milk pondered when I informed him of my plans to stop by Marcia and Markita's apartment. "What time she coming?"

"As soon as I call her."

"What time does the train leave?"

"I think 4:20."

"What time is it now?"

"Right at 4:00."

"Damn, nigga, when you coming back?"

Milk's attitude had changed after his injuries. For instance, the drinking and smoking that was never apart of his life before, was a constant. He also chased more skirts than he had before his injuries. It was like he was determined to enjoy the college experience of drinking drugging and sexing.

The apartment I lived in was a five minute walk from The Estes, which was right across the street from The Amtrak station, so I had a few minutes. I just had to make sure my female friend Crystal was coming. I had told her when I gave her my five-month old son to watch, that she was suppose to be ready to bring him to me right after the game was over. I just had to make it to my apartment, which was also close to the stadium, to get my bags and call her.

"She's on her way," I said to Milk as he rolled up the stashed away blunt cigar. "Hurry up, I want to hit that shit before I get on the train."

My son had been in Warrensburg for about two weeks. I was missing him real bad, so I made an Amtrak trip to St. Louis to get him for a week and he ended up staying two weeks. It was cool, though because my friend Crystal and my roommates helped me care for him the entire time he was there.

"T.P., when you say you was coming back?" Milk asked after toting the blunt a few times.

"I'm coming back tomorrow night with Ray and A.B.," I said, referring to Ray Lingard and Anthony Badlinger, two ex-Mule defensive backs who had finished their eligibility my red-shirt year. I had lined up a ride with them before the beginning of the Mo. Southern game. "They were at the game, but they left at halftime."

"That's cool," Milk said, passing the hocus-pocus. "I'll be right on that Amtrak Tuesday."

"Whatta mean?" I asked inquisitively.

"I got a doctor's appointment Tuesday afternoon, so I'll be on the train Tuesday morning. I'm trying to see if they gonna release me, so I can play this year."

Milk surprised me. I mean, I knew he still wanted to play ball, but with his hands being as limp as they were, I figured he would try to come back the following season. I was wrong and I'm sure Rod Smith's exploits that day made Milky even more anxious to get back on the field.

"We should have been out there, today, T.P.," Milk said before I got in Crystal's car with my son. "He wouldn't have got that shit off, I'm telling you, nigga. We would have shut that shit down."

Whatever the case, I ended up missing the ride back to Warrensburg with Ray and AB the Sunday after I touched down in St. Louis. I chalked it up to a communication breakdown, but either way, I was stranded in St. Louis because no one in my family had money to send me back on the train.

I wasn't on the team so I couldn't call Coach Noland, Hulet or our defensive coordinator Jeff Floyd. I tried asking Moody and Sean Mac for money the Monday after the Mo. Southern game, but they were busted, too. Moody said his mother would buy me a ticket if I was still in St. Louis that Wednesday because that's when she got paid. So with no other alternative, I was stranded in St. Louis until at least Wednesday evening.

That Monday evening, after getting off the phone with Moody's mother to set up our meeting later that week, I started reading a book called **Monster Cody** to kill time.

It was about a Cali gang-banger who had went to prison, redeemed himself and decided to write a memoir about his gangbang days and reformation. It was a powerful book.

Considering the fact the STL was in a full-fledged gang war itself, the book shed insight on some of the gang factions that had infiltrated The Lou in the late 1980's.

I ended up reading half the book that night. I woke up the following morning to finish the other half of the book. By Tuesday afternoon, I was restless, so I took a nap.

I woke up about a quarter to 5 p.m. and immediately went into my Grandma's kitchen to catch the KMOV evening news, which I hadn't seen since I left for fall semester in Warrensburg.

As the 4:58 p.m. news teaser came on that September 30th day, the broadcaster boldly stated "a 20-year old college student from Central Missouri State has been shot in the 5900 block of Garesche…"

My heart floored. My mouth dropped. In the midst of my own self-wallowing, I had forgotten Milk told me he was coming home Tuesday morning to see the doctor for clearance to play. I knew Milk lived on Garesche.

I remembered he was coming home, but I was still in denial. But, who else, besides me, would be home in the middle of the week from Central Missouri State.

I waited on the subsequent newscast. They gave me all the info I needed to know that my homeboy had been shot again. They didn't say his name, but they did say he was in critical condition.

I picked up the phone to call Moody and Sean Mac. No answer. I called the football offices for Coach Noland. No answer. Everybody was still at football practice or getting ready to go to the dining room. Either way, I had to get in contact with somebody on the team.

As I waited for numerous phone calls to be returned, my mother and I were standing on my Grandma's front porch when she noticed the strain on my face.

"What's wrong, baby," my concerned mother asked. "What happened?"

"Mama, I think they just shot my friend," I calmly reflected. "I think they got him."

"Your friend?" Moms politely asked. "What friend?"

"My friend I play ball with up at Central."

"They killed him?"

"Naw, he ain't dead, but I was watching Channel 4 and they said a twenty-year college student from Central Missouri State is in critical condition...."

"He got shot in St. Louis....what was he doing here if he was suppose to be at school?"

"Naw, mama, he came home to go to the doctor because they had already shot him this summer...."

"Who is they?"

"Don't nobody know, mama, we never asked him what happened the first time, but I it's probably the same people...I know it is. I think they got him this time, mama...I they killed my homie."

A million and one things happened between the 5 and 6 o'clock newscast that evening. Moody had called back and said Coach Noland had made the team aware of the situation. Moody told me to just sit back and wait on the word. His mother still was going to get me a ticket back to The 'Burg, but he wanted me to be cool in the meantime.

"They done took another one of our soldiers, T.P.," Moody said before excusing himself to be with Ping, Big Mo, Sean Mac, our freshmen homeboy from Tulsa, Oklahoma—Marcus Carlis--and the others. "My mother gonna have that ticket for you tomorrow, so just lay low until she get down to the City."

The 6 o'clock news was a crusher. The news anchor started the broadcast with an update on Milk: "That twenty-year-old college student we told you about at five has died from his injuries. Police has identified the victim as 20-year-old Wesley Maurice Drummond, a former all-metro football player at Parkway Central High…"

I couldn't believe what I heard. I had always thought that if you left the streets of St. Louis, you couldn't possibly die on the streets of St. Louis. Not a college student.

No way had I thought that could ever happen. It happened, though. It happened to my friend and teammate. It was definitely a wake-up call for me. Nobody seemed to care about the positives things we were trying to accomplish, especially in St. Louis. That's all that ran through my mind after Milk's death.

The City of No Luv. That was Milk's motto—St. Louis was The City of No Luv.

Things had changed drastically by the time I returned to Warrensburg that Thursday evening. The team had had a memorial service at The Chapel on campus the day before. Ping and Mo were among the hardest hit—they were Milk's roommates.

In an effort to keep the team focused on their upcoming game against Missouri Western State, Coach Noland decided against the team traveling to St. Louis for Milk's funeral, which was held the Friday after his death. Not only did I miss the memorial service on campus (I was still in St. Louis), I missed Milk's funeral in St. Louis. I got caught in-between and never got to see my homie laid to rest.

The Mules and Missouri Western played to a 14-14 tie that weekend, the first time Mo. West had ever played CMSU and didn't come away with a loss. The Mules would wind up 7-2-1 that season, missing the playoffs by one game. Some say, to a man, the Mo. West game is what caused the Mules to miss out on the school's first ever NCAA playoff berth that season.

The CMSU athletic department honored Milk after his death. They established an award called The Wesley Drummond Courage Award, which awards a plaque and game ball to the Mules' player who best represented Milk's courage, heart and determination. The award would be presented after every fourth game of the season (in case of a Mules' victory). The award is still presented to this day, nearly 15 years after Milk passed away.

We all still miss you, homie. See you in that Big End-Zone behind them Gates. You are truly our angel.

....reprinted from the St. Louis Post-Dispatch March 13, 1997

VIOLENT DEATHS: North St. Louis County: **Antonio Wadlington**, 21, was found stabbed to death about 4 a.m. Wednesday in his home in the 9600 block of Jacobi Avenue in the Castlepoint area of North County. **Wadlington**'s body was found by his girlfriend as she returned home from work. Robbery did not appear to be the prime motive.--*Copyright 1997 St. Louis Post-Dispatch*

THE CITY OF NO LUV, PART II

"That's my boy, that's my boy," an excited Antonio "Tony" Wadlington said to me while catching a glimpse of an ESPN Thursday Night football game.

The University of Tennessee was making one of their many national television appearances that 1995 season and Tony was stoked about the plays his friend and former Coffeyville Community College teammate, Leonard Little, was making for the Volunteers. "Look at him. That nigga's a beast, I'm telling you."

Seems Tony and old Leonard were buddies at the two-year school in Kansas prior to their stints at traditional four-year educational posts. Tony enrolled to play football at Coffeyville in the fall of 1994. He had just finished his senior year at Berkeley High School, where the St. Louis Suburban Journals named him their athlete of the year for his exploits in football, basketball and track during the 1993-94 school campaign. His plan was to attend Coffeyville for one year before he enrolled at Central Missouri State the following year.

Football coaches at CMSU had recruited Tony tough throughout his senior year at Berkeley. They liked his athleticism and toughness. The trash talking left a little to be desired. When it was time for Tony to take his recruiting trip to Warrensburg, the top brass at CMSU made me his recruiting host. My job was to make sure he had a good time and sell the university and its football program as a place to be.

CMSU wasn't a bad place to be in the early nineties if partying and bullshitting were the focal point. In terms of the football program, the Mules had fallen slightly off the top perch of the Mid-America (then Mid-Missouri) Athletic Association despite winning or sharing three MIAA championships from 1987-89. Still, the Mule Mystique reigned, so I figured the best way to get a an athlete the caliber of Tony Wadlington to sign with the Mules was to show him a good time in the humble city of Warrensburg.

To be honest, much of Tony's recruiting trip is a blur to me. I mean, I know we were prohibited by laws, rules and morals, but we—meaning—me, a few teammates, a couple of my roommates and a host of recruits—got pissy drunk, super high and chased a few skirts at an on-campus party. Tony excused himself once to go hurl, but other than that, a good time was had by all. CMSU had their man as Tony pledged his non-binding verbal agreement the day after the boozed-out, drug-fueled party crashing ordeal.

By the time I ran into Tony again--some six months later--things had changed. For starters, I had gotten expelled from CMSU because of bad grades and behavior issues and Tony was headed to Coffeyville for an abbreviated stop to work on his grades for NCAA eligibility before heading off to Warrensburg.

"Tony!" I screamed thru the thunderous beat of loud, angst-filled hip-hop music at The Palace Skating Rink, circa August 1994. "What's up, dawg? What's up with you?"

"Who that?" a sly looking Tony said, filtering through the well-wishes, glad-hands and back-pats reserved for athletes of his stature. "Who that?"

"Tory, nigga," I deadpanned. "Tory Porter from Central Missouri State. I was your recruiting host."

"Ahh, what's up, T." he shot back, laughing at the obvious mention of CMSU and his infamous up-chuck incident. "What's good with it, homeboy?"

"Nothing, chilling," I coolly countered. "What's up with you?"

"Man, nothing--just chilling with a couple of my homeboys."

"So, what's up, you still going to Central?"

"Yeah, I'm going. I gotta go to juco first, but I'm still going."

"Aw yeah? What juco you going to."

"Coffeyville. It's in Kansas."

"Nigga, I know where Coffeyville at. They be sending hella cats D-I, though.

"Yeah, man, I know, but I'm still coming up there."

"You know, I ain't going back to Central either this year."

"Oh yeah? Why not."

"Grades. Motherfuckas sent me back here on the first thang smokin'. But it's all good, though, I might go back next year.

"Aww T, you gotta make it happen, dirty. You one of the reasons I even wanna go up there"

"No doubt, no doubt—but, look, I'ma let you get back to yo' people. I'ma catch you before you leave and grab yo' number."

"Aw'ight, dirty. Be peaceful."

"Aw'ight, be peaceful."

True to his word, Tony enrolled at CMSU in the fall of 1995, a year after attending Coffeyville. I spent the 1994-95 academic year getting my ship in order at Harris-Stowe State College (now University) in St. Louis and Jefferson Junior College in Hillsboro, Missouri. Neither of those schools had football programs.

I re-enrolled at CMSU the summer of 1995. When two-a-day practices rolled around in August, Tony was there indeed. The bond was forged. The friendship solidified.

"I told ya'll niggas, my nigga is a beast," Tony said, continuing his Thursday night pro-Leonard Little tirade. We were on a fifteen minute break from the mandatory study hall implemented by the CMSU football staff and administration. Tony spent at least ten of those minutes big-upping Leonard Little and their Coffeyville days together.

"He going to the league," Tony proudly stated about the football tackling machine sporting the #1 orange Volunteer jersey. "I'm telling you, my nigga going to the league." Little, of course, wound up a Pro Bowl defensive end for the St. Louis Rams.

Tony had a pretty decent season for the Mules in '95. I had to sit out again that season because of transfer issues—essentially redshirting for the second time in my three-year Mules' career, which up to that point had spanned several big play practices, outstanding inter-squad scrimmages, grueling off-season workouts, devastating school expulsions, dream smashing athletic ineligibility and dire second chance opportunities. Everything except actual game day competition.

I enjoyed watching Tony's attempts to become a regular contributor at wide receiver for the Mules. Although he wasn't a standout gridiron performer, Tony flashed enough big-play potential that

Coach Terry Noland and staff entrusted him to handle punt and kick return duties in '95. He did a somewhat modest job on kick-off returns, but those punt returns were merely adventures. True he had speed to burn, but those hands were a bit unsteady fielding the rock.

Tony was disappointed he didn't do more on the field for the Mules and his grades suffered. At the end of the 1995-1996 academic year Tony Wadlington was out of a scholarship and back home living with his mother in Berkeley, Missouri.

During the summer of 1996, Tony made several trips to Warrensburg to visit friends and teammates. He usually stayed with me and my roommates in the three-bedroom apartment we shared off-campus. The gatherings consisted mainly of a lot of basketball, booze and bud. From time to time I would coyly slide in the conversations the fact I too lost my MuleBall scholarship in 1992, got sent home in 1994 and came back in 1995.

Tony often talked about going to Flo Valley Community College to get his grades up. He wanted to re-enroll at CMSU for spring semester 1997--go through the rigors of winter workouts and spring ball to earn his scholarship back. He promised he would attend all Mule home games in '96 to show support for both me and the program. I just so happened to get on a game day college field for the first time in '96.

A strange thing happened that 1996 season. Our head coach, Coach Noland was told he wasn't going to be retained after the season—a season that saw the Mules post the second of back to back four win seasons. There were three games left when CMSU athletic director Jerry Hughes broke the news to Coach Noland. Noland, a coach at CMSU for 14 seasons and owner of three MIAA championship rings, was floored. He abruptly left his position rather than coach the last three games as a 'lame duck' coach. Defensive coordinator Jeff Floyd finished the season coaching the Mules.

Coach Noland's departure created a mini-lull in the Mules' football program prior to the spring semester of 1997. Although new head coach Willie Fritz was bringing with him to CMSU a proven resume—his previous team at Blinn Junior College in Brenham, Texas had just won back to back national JUCO titles by going a combined 22-0 in 1995 and 1996—he had no clue about Tony Wadlington or his desire to return to CMSU.

Caught in between the pinch, Tony decided to stay in the St. Louis area for the spring '97 semester as well. Tony's plan was to re-enroll at Central for summer school after the semester ended and compete for time during summer workouts in Warrensburg.

Things were looking up for the Mules early in 1997. The effervescent Fritz had just got to town with him an impressive array of talented JUCO performers who helped him win those two national championships at Blinn. For me, I used the opportunity to learn from a coach who had put several players in the NFL. For Tony, it made him wish he was still in the 'Burg.

All in all, I was Tony's inside man on the new coach and I was the new coach's unwitting recruiter, constantly lecturing to Tony about why he needed to return to CMSU to play under Fritz.

I was on my way to another one of Fritz' invigorating winter workouts prior to spring practice when one of Tony's former freshmen cohorts at Central, Durand McNutt, ran up to me outside of the football offices. He delivered a crushing bit of news.

"T.P., you heard about the homeboy?" Durand said, barely audible through his grief stricken speech.

"What homeboy?" I fringed, "what'chu talking about?"

"Tony, man," Durand informed, "they found him last night dead, man. He was all stabbed up and shit."

"What!" I beckoned, damn near letting the knee buckling news take me down to the ground. "Dawg, don't tell me that."

Durand went on to provide the few details he knew of the circumstances behind Tony's brutal murder. He left me with the telephone number to his good friend Zell, who had attended both Berkeley High and CMSU with Tony. I immediately went to Fritz and his staff with the news.

They obliged my request to take the rest of the afternoon off. The gesture meant a lot to me for I never really got a chance to completely sell Fritz on Tony.

Zell basically told me Tony had been the victim of a botched robbery in the one-bedroom apartment Tony shared with his girlfriend in the Castle Point neighborhood of North St. Louis County.

The intruders had tied Tony up, Zell informed, stabbed him several times and shot him in the head.

"Look, T.P.," Zell advised through the long-distance phone call from Warrensburg to St. Louis. "I'ma holla at Tony's old gal and see when the funeral is and I'ma call you and let you know."

"Damn dirty, that's fucked up," I petitioned to Zell.

"I know, T.P." Zell countered. "But I'ma find out what's good and hit you back."

"Aw'ight. One."

"One."

Zell called me back a somber day and a half later with even more distressing news.

"Hey, T.P.," Zell spilled, "look, man you might as well don't even come to St. Louis, dawg. Tony's old gal, she hurting dawg. She ain't even having a funeral from him, dirty. She just gon' cremate his body and have a lil' sumthin' for him."

I can't summon, or for one instant, imagine the pain of burying a son, so I completely understood Tony's mother's decision. I just wished I would have gotten a chance to tell her how important her son was to a lot of people. I wanted her to know how his charm, wit and athleticism impacted a diverse amount of people. I wanted to tell her sorry for being the cohort who entertained those girls with booze and bud in their house in Berkley that weekend in July '96 when she went out of town with her husband. Damn, Tony Wad--we had a ball that day man, we had a ball. We ran through a half-ounce of bud, downed a fifth of Hennessey and watched your girlfriend and her cousin on leave from the military fight our two female friends from Central. I'll never forget that day, dude, and you'll never be forgotten. See you when I get there.

...reprinted from the St. Louis Post-Dispatch May 30, 1994...

CHEERS, TEARS MARK DAY OF SUPERLATIVES AND BIT OF SADNESS

By Kevin E. Boone of the Post-Dispatch

...Saturday was a day for track and field superlatives: Most Starry-eyed: Berkeley freshman Terrell Brown ran legs on the triumphant 4x100- and 4x400-meter relay teams... "It was my dream to run on a state-championship team and to run on the same (4x100) relay team with (senior) **Tony Wadlington**. He's my idol."--*Copyright 1994 St. Louis Post-Dispatch*

...reprinted from the St. Louis Post-Dispatch April 23, 1999...

LAW & ORDER

Teen is killed in shooting

Courtney Bradley, 18, was fatally shot and two of his friends wounded Thursday night in a shooting in the 4100 block of Flad Avenue. **Bradley**, who lived in north St. Louis County, was shot in the throat. He died in the emergency room of an area hospital.--*Copyright 1999 St. Louis Post-Dispatch*

SHED SO MANY TEARS

It's really sad when violence and death starts to become commonplace in life. Imagine for a second the life you live—no matter how peaceful or pleasant--being turned upside down because of senseless murder after senseless murder.

I had escaped the so-called mean streets of my hometown of St. Louis during The City's Generation X influenced bang-bang, shoot 'em up phase of the 1990's for the safer pastures of a fine institute of higher learning located in Warrensburg, Missouri. Needless to say, violent death is not supposed to find you in a square-peg town like Warrensburg, home of Central Missouri State University.

No matter how harsh the laws are enforced in the rural in-skirts of Johnson County, Missouri, murder is the unthinkable, the unconscionable. Then again, life is what it is. If the spirits move where they move, hell, they move. Although I never lost anyone close to me in the actual city of Warrensburg, the old grim reaper has made it known---some 200 miles and a mere phone call away—remnants of death knows no boundaries.

First there was Milk, a St. Louis native who left St. Louis for college in Warrensburg. Milk played football for the Mules. His claim to fame—never mind he was an all-district football player at Parkway Central High in the early 90's—was he blew Rod Smith's knee out when Rod Smith was a junior in college. Rod Smith, to the uninitiated, is a All-Pro wide receiver and 12-year vet for the NFL's Denver Broncos.

Milk got killed in October of 1993 in St. Louis a few blocks from his family's residence in the Walnut Park area of The City. He was in St. Louis from school to visit a doctor for whom Milk wanted approval to begin playing football again. Gunshot wounds from a July '93 incident left his hands partially paralyzed and Milk needed the doctor's clearance to play. The perpetrators, whom many believed were involved in the earlier shooting, killed Milk the second time around.

Then there was my younger cousin Lil' Damon. Lil' Damon was only 18-years-old when they found him dead from a gunshot wound to the head on a vacant lot on Park Avenue near where I grew up in South St. Louis. I had just seen Lil' Damon a month before his death while I was home for a week-long spring break vacation from CMSU. I tried to convince him to visit the peaceful oasis, but he didn't bite.

Nearly four weeks later I got the news of his fate. Both of them were among the 274 murders committed in the City of St. Louis during its record-setting campaign of 1993. Lil' Damon was homicide victim #64. Milk was #197.

After that, it was the big homie Meko. Meko died in the early parts of January 1994 when a STLPD officer shot him in the head during a drug raid. I was in--what else but—Warrensburg when I got wind of Meko's passing.

How about Tony Wadlington? Tony was a three-sport athlete at Berkeley High in suburban St. Louis when he high-tailed it to Coffeyville College in Kansas in 1994 to play football. After a year in the middle of the Sunflower State, Tony enrolled at CMSU, just in time for fall semester 1995. He played in all 11 football games for the Mules that season before being sent home for insufficient progress toward graduation. In March 1997, his girlfriend found him dead in the apartment they shared. A mutual friend called me from St. Louis with the tragic information. I, again, was ducked off in Warrensburg trying to escape the madness of the streets when I got the call.

Even still, with all the preparation one could possibly need, I was still dropped to my knees when yet another haunting call came in from St. Louis to Warrensburg the morning of April 23rd, 1999.

A close friend, Rory L. Watkins, and I had just celebrated my son, Toriano II's 6th birthday the day before. The plan was to keep celebrating on the 23rd because it was my oldest brother--who had been locked up since 1993--Bean Pole's birthday. Bean Pole was confined to the state penitentiary in Jefferson City so Nose—Rory's nickname—and I poured a little liquor for him, Lil'T. and the rest of our family, friends and wayward souls who weren't able to join us.

My cousin Carlyle, who had left for the Marines a month after his 1992 high school graduation, called from his locale in St. Louis with the bereaved news of his younger brother Courtney Bradley.

Seems Courtney and his partner had had a physical beef with some guys from a rival North St. Louis neighborhood while in the rival's hood visiting a girl. Courtney and the friend supposedly got the best of the rivals in a fist-fight, so the rivals doubled back a few hours later on Courtney and his pals in their South St. Louis hut. The resulting gunfire claimed Courtney's life at an all too precious 18-years-old.

I, along with Nose and Lil' T, who were both living with me in Warrensburg at the time, packed some belongings and logged the three-and-a half hour drive down Interstate 70 (by way of Missouri Highway 13) from the 'Burg to St. Louis after the news of Courtney's fatality.

We attended the wake and subsequent funeral. After paying our proper respects to the family, we departed back for the friendly confines of College Town, USA.

The hardest part of Courtney's passing away ceremony was witnessing the sheer pain of not only his mother and step-father, but his father Bo Jack's pain, his brothers' Carlyle, Cornell and Cedric's pain and his sister Tonya's pain, as well as the pain of other family members and friends. People were really distraught over Courtney's passing, as they should be for anyone dying that violently that young.

For that, I wish I would have never gotten that all too disturbing phone call from Carlyle. C-Murder, we all know you had to go, but why did you have to go so soon? You had so much more to give than what you gave in those eighteen shortened years. We miss you, and we'll see you again real soon. Shine brightly on all who've known you.

.....reprinted from the St. Louis Post-Dispatch March 9, 2004.....

Woman is charged with killing boyfriend

Jacqueline Neal, 25, was charged Monday with second-degree murder in the fatal shooting of her boyfriend, **Julius Eberhart** , 32, St. Louis police said.

Neal told homicide detectives the shooting happened about 9:45 p.m. Sunday during a quarrel in a car as **Eberhart** was driving on Interstate 70 near West Florissant Avenue, police said.

Neal said **Eberhart** had pulled out a pistol during the quarrel but later placed it on the seat. She said she then picked it up, police reported. Neal said that as she was holding the gun, a vehicle struck their car in the rear, causing the pistol to discharge, police said.-- *Copyright (c) 2004 St. Louis Post-Dispatch*

SHED SO MANY TEARS, PART II

"Nigga, you can't hoop," I teased an old friend nearly ten years after our last encounter. The friend, Julius Eberhart, had wandered, quite aimlessly, into the convenience store my family owned on the City's Southside, sorting through an array of over the counter goodies and cakes, obviously oblivious to my presence.

"Toriano?" JuJu enthusiastically said after realizing the subject of his impromptu ribbing. "Hell naw! Man, what'chu you doing in herre?"

"Man, this my people's spot," I said shortly after an empathetic handshake/hug. "I'm here damn near everyday."

JuJu was a standout basketball player throughout his younger days playing for the St. Louis Zips, a 1980's staple in the annals of youth basketball programs in St. Louis. By the time the Carr Square Village reared ball hawk got to Eureka High as a sophomore he was a combination guard/small forward with deft ball handling skills and uncanny scoring ability. His defense, according to our sophomore coach, Craig Kennedy, left a little to be desired. His offensive capabilities were more than enough to atone for any of JuJu's defensive liabilities.

Coach Kennedy regular chided JuJu about his defensive shortcomings. Coach would constantly question JuJu's commitment to defensive excellent—our sophomore squad was built on speed, defensive pressure and smarts—but nonetheless place the enigmatic JuJu among the first five game after game. JuJu had mad game and Coach K knew it. In fact, JuJu was even getting looked at by Coach Gene Myers for possible varsity playing time.

"Damn, JuJu," I continued after our heart-felt embrace, "where you been, man."

"Man, I been around," he said, steady searching for some mid-afternoon snacks. "Where you been? Nigga, I ain't seen you in hellas."

"Shiiidddd, man," I countered, "I been around."

JuJu and I jaw-jacked a few more minutes before the young lady he was riding with came into the store. She was a bit annoyed.

"Damn, JuJu," the portly-shaped woman screamed, "what's taking you so long?"

"Damn, baby, chill out," JuJu shot back, "I'm in herre hollin' at my homeboy from high school."

JuJu, smoothing over the slight episode, casually introduced me to the woman--his girlfriend and mother of JuJu's two kids. He paid for the snacks and sent his girl back to the car before going down memory lane.

"T, remember when we played The V our sophomore year," JuJu chimed, "and we had that two-on-one fast break?" The V— as in national basketball powerhouse Vashon High, as well as local power DeSmet High's "B" teams were two of the teams on our sophomore team's 1989-90 schedule.

Coach Kennedy was enthused about the sophomore class of 1992 from both Rockwood South and Eureka Junior Highs. Rockwood South and Eureka Jr. were both feeder schools to Eureka Sr. High at the time. The gig was Coach Kennedy's first boy's basketball job after coaching the girl's varsity at Eureka a couple of seasons prior to '89. He challenged his talented collection of athletes by assembling a schedule that featured some of the area's better basketball programs.

"You remember that shit?" I asked JuJu about the distant memory of him and me running one of Coach K's fundamental fast breaks.

JuJu, based on his Carr Square Village roots, resided within The V's boundaries. He dreamed of donning the Wolverine Blue and White of The V, but his mother had other plans. She enrolled JuJu and his siblings in the voluntary desegregation program. JuJu, like most of us from the City, had trouble adjusting to the rural aspects of Eureka, Mo, but somehow still managed to enjoy the daily 30 mile excursion.

"Man, we straight beat them cats that day," JuJu exclaimed about the mild upset. His former Zips teammate, Jermaine "Q-Ball" Kemp, had told JuJu all week long how Kemp and his Vashon "B" team comrades were "gonna kill ya'll white boys."

We beat both The V and DeSmet that year, finishing a respectable 18-6 before heading for the varsity team the following year. "Them niggas was talkin' all shit, too," JuJu continued.

We wrapped up our nostalgic based conversation by exchanging contact information. JuJu wanted to know — and me to prove — if I still had some basketball skills. He assured me he hadn't lost his touch.

"We gon' go hoopin' Monday," JuJu boastfully promised, doubting my claims I still had it, "and see what'chu got. Make sho' you call me Tory, man."

I watched JuJu out the door on that beautiful early spring Friday afternoon. I could see his still annoyed girlfriend...well...still annoyed. He flashed his trademark toothy grin through the front windshield at her as he approached the car. I laughed because I remembered the Rudolph Valentino type charm he displayed to the girls at Eureka back in the day. He and his girl kissed as they pulled off the lot and I laughed again. That big-headed fool has still got it, I thought.

It was business as usual the Monday after JuJu's visit to the store. In some ways it was fitting JuJu would come into my place of employment - after all, his brother Jason - a standout athlete in the late 1990's at Mehlville High School who later played defensive end on the 2001 University of Illinois football team that lost to LSU in the 2002 Sugar Bowl - Jason's girlfriend and Jason's girlfriend's younger brother Brandon - were regular patrons at the Porter family's gas filling establishment.

In fact, Brandon mentioned to me shortly after JuJu's visit that he didn't know I knew his "big brother". Three days later, Brandon dropped a load on me that reverberates numbing pain through my body to this day.

"Cuzz, JuJu dead," Brandon said to me as he approached the sales counter that Monday. Immediately my heart sank. "His gal shot him last night, cuzz, and killed him."

I was too distraught to make sense of the circumstances behind JuJu's death. Brandon tried explaining to me what had happened between JuJu and his girl, but the story was so unbelievably cruel I *couldn't* make sense of it.

"Man, you bullshiting!" was all I could muster.

JuJu's wake, funeral and going home celebration was difficult for me. I mean, here it was, a friend who I hadn't seen in nearly a decade, dead because of a domestic dispute (his girl was charged with involuntary manslaughter) merely three days after our post-high school real world encounter. I shed many tears as they laid my Homie to rest.

JuJu you left this place a legend from a legendary family. Your kids will continue to live on in your legacy. God knew I needed an angel in my life so he sent you to see me before your homecoming. I'm glad I knew you. You will be sorely missed.

…reprinted from the St. Louis Post Dispatch February 25, 2008.…

St. Louis city police have identified the victims of the latest two homicides…In a homicide from Friday, police say, **Rory Watkins** was shot several times in the head as he sat in a car in the 4100 block of West Lee Avenue.

Police say **Watkins** was sitting in a car when he was shot about 10:45 a.m. Friday. Witnesses told police they heard three gunshots and saw a man run away.—*Copyright 2008 St. Louis Post-Dispatch*

Shed So Many Tears, Part III

Dedicated to my best friend and brother-at-arms Rory L. Watkins, Big Ant, Chicken and PeeWee Lindsey, Victor Harper, "Sleep Dog" Curry aka Courtland Martin, Uncle Meechie, my precious Great Grandma Nanna, my lifeblood Martha Gandy, Uncle Pat Gandy, Grandma McKinney, Stokley Thomas, Ramone Wright, Big Ernest Blackwell, Solo Da Hittman, Katt Davis, Rodney Sessions, Jasmine McKinney, Coach Dave Bassore and a host of family, friends and wayward souls who never got a chance to live out their dreams. Rest in Eternal Peace.

My Homie. My partner. My best friend. My brother is gone.

When I got the word that my best friend of nearly 23 years was gunned down in cold blood in the streets of St. Louis, I was devastated. It was and always will be the saddest day of my life.

I mean, damn, me and my dude had so much we wanted to do with this writing. He had all these wonderful tales he wanted to share and I wanted to help him share them.

I'm dedicated to that mission. Every time I sit down to write, I'm dedicating it to the realest brother I have ever known, Rory L. Watkins, forever and always known as O.G. Nose from Laclede Town's Lawton Block.

A father of three, a friend of many and one of a kind, I met my dude the first day of our 6th grade year and we have been partners in crime, brothers at arms and kindred spirits since. We will survive.

Nose, your memory lives on. I could not, for the life of me, muster the strength or the courage to write your eulogy, bro. The pain is still fresh. You are gone and it hurts too bad.

Know that I love you, I miss you and I pray everyday for your spirit to protect me and guide me as it did when you were here. You are truly one of my guardian angels.

SECTION II

SHORT STORIES,
FLASH FICTION AND MORE

The Swinging Gate featuring Rory L. Watkins

No Ordinary Day featuring Rory L. Watkins

Straddlin' the Fence

More Colors

Straddlin' the Fence, Part II

Five Deep

A Place Where Hoop Dreams Dare To Live

A Mighty Fine Introduction

She's Got It

Three Month Fling (You Lousy Son of Bitch)

General Isaiah

April's Nobody's Fool

Age Ain't Nothing But a Number, Right?

With or Without The Ring

The Evening Whirl

Background Check

The Pride of St. Louis

THE SWINGING GATE
FEATURING RORY L. WATKINS

Cassius Clay Winston circa 1985:

Yesterday was a strange day. Even though it was kinda strange, it was sorta fun. It was the first day of the new school year and I was headed to a new school, Eureka Elementary. I woke up yesterday morning at five o'clock, but I wasn't mad or tired or nothing. I was excited and could not wait to catch the bus at six. My mother Moms was up with me and my big brother Sonnie.

As you can tell Moms is a BIG boxing fan. Anyways, like I was saying, me and Sonnie woke up, took our wash up, brushed our teeth, and ironed our clothes. Moms took us school shopping Saturday, so we were trying to be nice and clean for the new kids we didn't know yet. Sonnie was funny. He was the reason why we couldn't go to Columbia Middle School. He kept saying yesterday to Moms "I'on wanna go to that white school, I'on wanna go to that white school." I was thinking 'fool, you the reason we going to that white school.'

See, we used to live on the Southside of The City and had seen a few white people, but our neighborhood was all black. Then we moved to the JVL. The Jeff Vanderlou projects that is. The JVL is on the Northside of The City and we have been having problems with the JVL Posse. I'on know why they don't like us, but they don't. Them cats look very scary. Sonnie wants to take 'em all on and I'm like 'they cool, they ain't said nothing to me.' See, Sonnie went to Columbia Middle last year and I went to Dunbar Elementary and me and some of those JVL guys were real good friends. And I know for a fact they were in the JVL posse.

But Sonnie got into it with one of them older cats on the last day of school and they been looking for him all summer long. He stayed with my grandmother Grandma on the Southside all summer so they haven't caught him yet. Moms knew some of the people in the neighborhood and they told her the JVL Posse was looking for Sonnie so she made us transfer schools out to the county.

I was mad at first because I wanted to go to Columbia. People was saying how much fun it was. I guess I'll never know.

So, anyways, when me and Sonnie got to the bus stop yesterday I saw some of my friends from Dunbar on their way to Columbia and they were looking at us crazy and mean. I just saw them cats a week ago and we played cork ball together on the Church lot and everything was cool, so when I saw them I was like 'what's up, Darius, Marcus, Baby?' and they just looked and stared.

Sonnie just stared back, grabbed me by the back of the neck and said "C'mon little brother, I got you." I really don't know what happend between my brother and the JVL Posse, but I get the feeling Sonnie don't like them cats too much. I was really glad when our bus came, because Darius 'nem was tripping off me and my brother's new shoes Moms had got us at the mall Saturday and I thought we was gonna have to fight. And man, I hate fighting. I just wanna play ball and live good like Ozzie, Vince and Willie.

The morning kept getting weirder. The bus pulled up and the bus driver asked me for my bus pass. He looked at it and said "Wrong, bus little guy, you have to wait on the other bus." I was like "what other bus?" "The one that says Eureka Elementary, this bus here is for the junior and senior highs." I looked at Sonnie, Sonnie looked at me and we both looked at Darius 'nem. "You'll be alright little brother, they yo' partners right?" Sonnie got on the bus. I wasn't scared but I was.

Darius, Marcus and Baby had always been cool with me but they hated my brother, so I was kinda nervous. They just started asking all sort of questions out of the clear blue sky like "Why ya'll ain't going to Columbia, Cass? Where you get them shoes at Cass? Where dat 'foxy momma of yours at, Cass?"

And then the bus came.

Cochise Williams circa 1985:

Yesterday was my first day at my new elementary school. I was one of many proud Afro-Americans who were chosen to be a part of the St. Louis City and County desegregation program.

I was just one of about fifty of us coming here to Eureka from the city. The long wait for a lot of us is over and we are glad as heck to finally be bussed out here to a county school. We all was excited and screaming on the bus talking about how much we was going to learn and how many new friends we was going to meet. I know I hated waking up so early to catch the bus and ride some twenty miles just to go to school.

For the most part, the inner city kids have open minds. Nobody on the bus was talking about "kill whitey!" or nothing like that. We was just happy that our teachers was going to be friendly and want to help us learn. At least that's what my mother told me.

Most of the kids in this class, oops, I mean our class, were white and that was new to me, but they were all pretty cool. I even met a friend on the bus and when I got to school. One is black and the other one is white, but I don't care, that's why my mother sent me and my brothers and sister out here, to meet new friends and see different things and how different people live.

It was kind of cool to be in a classroom with carpet on the floor and new textbooks. The cafeteria even served good food and the gym was spanking new. The inner city kids was glad to be in better surroundings I can tell you that. That's all mugs kept talking about on the bus ride home. The gym. The cafeteria. The teachers nice and smart and they care.

Now I'm not going to lie. It got kind of crazy in my gym glass. This one student, I hate to call him a white boy, but he is white, cried the whole time and I couldn't figure out why. Not at least until Dirk Lauderhill told me that the dude was crying because his family is racist and they scared of black people and the dude was uncomfortable around us. I thought no way, but Dirk kept saying it was true.

No Ordinary Day featuring Rory L. Watkins

St. Louis, MO--**August 1990**--Cochise and Cass had been friends for years so it was no surprise when Cochise called his buddy to let him in on the good news.

"Cass, dirty," Cochise screamed into the phone. "Guess what?"

Cass, still half-sleep, was shook up. "Who is this?" he stubbornly asked.

"This Chedda, fool," Cochise remarked.

"Chedda Chise," Cass acknowledged. "What's up, homie?"

"Man, today's my brother birthday," Cochise excitedly said, "and he's 'bout to comp a new swerve."

Cass was a bit confused at first and then caught his wits. "Damn, today is the 23rd, ain't it? So what did he say?"

Cochise's older brother Big O.G. had told Cochise that he was buying a new car for himself on his birthday and Chise could use the 1988 Ninety-Eight Regency that Big O.G. had parked in the driveway of their mother's house. Big O.G. had never let anyone drive his Nine-Eight. Ever.

"He said I could get the keys as soon as he gets back from the car lot," Cochise exclaimed.

Cass was skeptical. "Dawg, you think he jeffin'?"

Big O.G.'s Nine-Eight wasn't just a regular old Nine-Eight. It was a baller's Nine-Eight. You know the kind; custom fifty spoke Dayton wire rims, 15-inch vogue tires, laid out bumper kit and a custom sunroof to show off the plush snowflake white leather interior. The leather interior matched the candy coated paint job on the Nine-Eight's pristine body.

Oh, I almost forgot about the JVC sound-system, with the four 6x9 speakers, crossover and amps and two fifteen inch subwoofers. How could I forget about the beats?

"He chunked it up on the 'hood, he wasn't jeffin'," Cochise replied, "so, dirty, be ready when I get there."

"When you coming," Cass asked looking for a watch, clock or something.

"I'on know," Cochise answered, "probably around noon time."

"What time is it now," Cass wanted to know, not knowing he was setting himself up to be the punch-line of another one of Cochise's silly antics.

"Half past the monkey's ass and a quarter to his nuts," Cochise teased, right before he delivered a piece of useful advice towards Cass. "Call time, fool or get a watch."

Before Cass could even muster a reply, Cochise hung up.

****

A few hours had elapsed since Cass and Cochise's conversation and Cass was getting restless. He picked up the phone to call Cochise, but was not so rudely interrupted.

"Boy, I'm on the damn phone," Cass' mother shouted from the living room of their government subsidized three-bedroom apartment, echoing through the phone wires and off the walls.

"Moms, my fault," Cass shot back, muttering damn under his breath for effect.

"Who are you talking to little boy," Moms chimed, disregarding whatever or whoever on the opposite phone line.

Cass and Moms had an understanding kind of relationship going on and he knew how to keep her off his back. For the most part that is.

"I was just saying, I'm sorry for picking up the phone," Cass explained. "But I was trying to call Chedda to see when he was coming to pick me up."

"Cochise?" Moms questioned. She was sort of dumbfounded. She knew that neither Cass nor

Cochise had a car or a driver's license. "Pick you up with what, the Bi-State?"

"No." Cass corrected. "Big O.G. is giving him the Nine-Eight for the day."

"Is that right?" Moms hastily reacted. "Cochise had better not have stolen another one of them cars again. And if he has, your ass ain't going nowhere."

"Moms, Big O.G. is buying a new car for his birthday and he gave Chedda the keys to the Nine-Eight," Cass explained. "Everything's cool."

Just as Moms raised her hand to counter Cass' explanation, they both turned their attention to the outside front and the loud thunderous noise booming through the neighborhood.

"I'ma call you back," Moms bellowed into the phone, oblivious to the caller's objection to the sudden lack of attention. "I said I'ma call you back."

The beats. Cass knew who it was.

"My homie," Cass said, opening the shades of the living room window while unlocking the front door at the same time. "Beatin' down the block, baby, beatin' down the block."

"Move," Moms shouted, shoving Cass to the side, preparing to lecture Cass' closest friend. "Bring your butt here Cochise, right now."

Moms was upset. She didn't mind Cochise coming to pick Cass up in Big O.G.'s car, but she was concerned about them flashing their newfound, albeit brief, glory.

"O.K., Moms let me park," Cochise responded.

"Little boy," Moms admonished Cochise as strutted his way toward Cass' residence, "you don't have to broadcast your arrival on this block. Your mere presence is sufficient enough. Do you know these guys will put a pistol to your head for hi-siding on them in their own backyard? You do know that don't you."

"Yes ma'am," Cochised admitted.

Moms usually gives it to you when she gives it to you, but Cochise had an innate ability to diffuse certain situations and he was an expert dealing with folk's parents. He was above average height, brown-skinned, mildly intelligent, street savvy and confident. Cass thought Cochise was a charming son of a gun. Cochise called it 'mad game.'

"O.K. I'ma leave it alone," Moms said, questioning Big O.G's rationale for giving Cochise the Nine-Eight.

"I have my permit already, Moms," Cochise said, giving Cass the winking eye. "But I'm 'bout to go to the license bureau right now to take my driver's test and you know I need Cass Money there with me for good luck."

"Hmmph," Moms sighed. "Boy that's a bold face lie, but oh well, if Big O.G. don't care, I surely don't. Ya'll just be careful. The police would love to take ya'll little black butts to the juvey center. And guess what, Cassius? I'm not coming to get you. Good day. Get out of my house."

Once in the ride, Cass couldn't believe Big O.G. had given up the Nine-Eight, but he wasn't going to complain. "Where we headed, Chedda?" Cass asked.

"To the license bureau," Cochise stated. "Why you ask?"

"Seriously, where are we headed, homie?" Cass wanted to know.

Cochise eased up on his story. "I'on know, fool, we just gonna' cruise the St. Louis streets, see what we see, do what we do and screw what we screw." Cass laughed. Cochise reached in the fold-down ashtray in the middle of the Nine-Eight's console and emerged with a bag full of funk.

"And blow our brains back."

Cass had seen marijuana before but he had never smoked it. (Actually, when Cass was nine-years-old, his favorite uncle, Moms' brother Unc, let Cass hit a joint a couple of times, but that's another story). "What's that for?" Cass nervously responded.

"To smoke and get high," Cochise wryly replied.

"I mean, I know that, but what do we need it for?" Cass protested.

"So we can ride out, smoke out, have some fun, pick up some hoochies and do how these cats with paper do. We some ballers today, dirty, me and you. Let's do the damn thing. We got the swerve, we got the beats, we got the herb and we got this," Cochise said, cocking the chrome .380 automatic pistol he sneaked from Big O.G.'s gun collection.

"Man," Cass relented, "Moms was right. We're going to jail tonight."

"Dirty, we good," Cochise retorted. "As long as I got the wheel, we straight, so roll up."

"I don't know how to roll that stuff, dawg, you tripping," Cass rebuffed.

"Ole' cry-baby, titty-licking, mama's boy, can't do nothin'," Cochise teased. "I'll roll it myself."

"Yeah, you do that," Cass said.

"I will," Cochise countered.

"Fine," Cass stood firm. "I still ain't smoking it."

"Yes you are," Cochise demanded.

"No, I ain't," Cass offered.

Cochise was getting aggravated by Cass' resistance so he turned the car's stereo system back to full blast, put the car in drive and peeled off.

"You smoking today," he said, ignoring Cass' pleas. Cochise emphasized his position by burning tire rubber on the neighborhood's black-tar asphalt while at the corner stop sign. "Yep, you getting blowed today, dirty, so don't even trip."

STRADDLIN' THE FENCE (PART I)

In these days and times, living that street life can become a wasted time of petty hustle and life-threaten situations. With gang-banging, dope-slanging, and pistol-popping at an all-time high, it's easy to see why The City has become a war zone.

It was in The City that I learned the instincts of survival and doing what had to be done to get ahead in life. Whether good or bad, survival, at least for me, was the key to all existence.

It was my 'hood in The City that promised to take me under. And it was The City's street life that I yearned and fiend for, but had to abandon.

Growing up as a teenager in The City, there were many choices I had to make: Do I slang dope? Gang-bang? Run the streets? or: Do I go to school? Play ball? Go to college? Do I even fool myself with the thought of going to college? Do I get a so-called honest job?

Me deciding on those choices, set the tone for my trials and tribulations through young adulthood.

I'd say I was generally a nice kid at about sixteen. I was damn near the only person on my block who was still in school. And I know for sure I was damn near the only person who didn't slang dope back then. Sports were my thing. Since I really didn't trip off sex like my partners did, playing ball was the only thing that got me excited. I did it all. Football, basketball, baseball--shit sports was my sex. I had had sex only once in my first sixteen years, so my partners used to tease me constantly about my lack of names on the infamous "Hood-Rat Hit List."

Especially Cochise.

Cochise was a cool ass cat. With that sleek, lean body forever gangsta' strutting, he made sure everyone knew he was cool, too. Everywhere he went, school (half the time), the basketball courts, even the corner store, he was always popping off at the mouth, starting static with anyone who questioned his coolness.

"Hey, cuzz," Cochise said to me a couple months into the new school year. He had stolen a 1987 Buick Regal and ridden it some 27 miles to school and convinced me to make a spontaneous dash to the local 7-11 for nachos and Big Gulps after school. "We've been in school foe' both two and a half months and you ain't even tried to talk to none of these hood-rat bitches. Nigga, is you gay or something'?"

"Naw, playboy," I said, trying to keep from laughing at the fool. "Playing ball my thang. I ain't tripping off none of these rats right now."

"Yeah, I know you ain't tripping off no rats, 'cause you gay."

"Naw, you tripping', dog. These rats can't do nothing' for me, right now. I want me a scholarship to college."

That wasn't the first time I had told someone I was going to get a scholarship to college. In fact, when I told people that, they'd just look at me and smile. Like I was telling a joke or something. Cochise was no different.

"Nigga, they ain't got no college for cats who don't get no booty," he teased. "What college you gon' go to? I Don't Have Sex State University'! Cassius, you a crazy dude."

"Man, I thought you played football," Cochise asked when I told him I was trying to get a baseball scholarship to college.

"I do. But I got more skills at baseball. Speaking of football, I got to go to practice, cuzz. Give me a ride back up to school!"

Cochise was the kind of cat who liked to see a person beg before he did something for them. That particular time, he tried to compromise.

"Aw'ight," he said, rolling his eyes and nodding his head as if to say 'Sucka!' "But you know chronic smokers are the only people allowed in my car? No squares. So, if you get back in you gon' hafta give me five on a dime sack, roll the blunt and smoke it with me. You down, cuzz?"

I couldn't believe my partner was really going to have me smoke weed before I went to football practice. I could tell by the way he said it, he was semi-serious.

"I ain't got no money, cuzz," I said, trying to whiff my way out of smoking weed. "Moms ain't got that welfare check, yet."

"Dawg, you a athlete! Tell dem crackers to start paying you. Shit, dem muthafuckas got to give you some grip if you ask for it. All of dat damn slavin' ya'll do foe 'em! You ever ask one of dem coaches for some money, cuzz?"

"Nope!"

"Cass, you a crazy dude. Get in the car."

Like I said, it was something about The City that I loved. Even though I went to school in The County, The City had all the action. Girls, money, weed (oh, I had changed dramatically from 16 to 17). It was all right there in The City.

At seventeen I still planned on going to college, but I had other interests--mainly a newfound fascination with girls, money, and weed. I was still damn near the only person on my block who went to school. But, I also started gang-banging, selling crack, messing with rats, and getting high. All this and still playing ball.

It was kind of hard to split time between school, ball, slanging, banging and messing with the rats. Something had to suffer and it was football at first.

The football coach came to me one day, lectured me, and kicked me off the team. Like I was criminal or something. He said something like ' I don't know what's wrong with you, son, but you've changed. You're not the same Cassius Clay Winston I know. My sources tell me you're a dope peddler now and I've got to rid my hands of you. Please get control of your life back.'

I sat there thinking. This is just an old fool talking about something he knew nothing about. After all, I had control of my life. Well, a person thinks like that when he's seventeen anyhow.

"Cassius," Moms screamed at me one day shortly after being kicked off the football squad. "This fool Cochise down here."

"O.K."

Moms was the type of mother who was more like a sister. The kind that thinks they're seventeen instead of thirty-seven.

She was a tall, toothpick built women, with a gold tooth smile that would light up my worst days.

She was mad cool. Almost like a sister. The only problem I ever had with Moms was that she depended on guys too much. She always felt like a man had to take care of her. In the times she didn't work --if she didn't have a boyfriend--our only support was welfare. I used to tell her all the time that she didn't need no man to take care of us, but with no money I was just talking.

When I started slanging dope, shit changed. Moms didn't seem to care less where I got money. She was just happy I was still going to school.

"What's up cuzz?" I said to Cochise as I walked down the steps.

"What you and Moms talkin' 'bout?"

"Nothing. She's trying to talk a brother into going back to school."

"Cassius," Moms said, "Tell that boy he needs to get back in school."

"Moms, I tell him everyday."

I had lined me and Cochise up with some rats from the Other Side of The City, so I figured we'd mess with them and come back and smoke some weed with Moms. After all she didn't have a job. She wasn't going anywhere.

"Hey, cuzz," Cochise said to me like a kid anticipating Christmas. "What rats you got us hooked up with?"

Boy! How things change so quickly. A year earlier, that same cat was the one teasing me about girls. It was also the same cat who had introduced me to every girl I had knew at that time. Now, I was the one hooking us up.

"These two rats from the Other Side," I said.

"What rats you talkin' 'bout? I ' on know 'bout goin' on the Other Side."

"Naw, Cochise, cuzz. We just gon' pick 'em up and get a hotel room. It's cool."

"I' on know, Cochise warned, "dem cats been trippin' lately, cuzz. Dem fools blasted on a cat last night visiting his mama. His mama, nigga. Shot him three times in the chest! I'm sho' glad I packed my pistol."

The Other Side of the The City was where most of This Side of The City enemies lived. Both sides were wild and crazy. My neighborhood was on This Side. This Side was rough, but The Other Side was just as violent.

"You ain't gon' even need that pistol, cuzz," I said to Cochise as we headed toward the Other Side. "I'll promise you we in and out in a minute."

"And then we headed to the telly? I'ma hold you to dat," Cochise said, winking at me.

When I said The City was a war zone, I wasn't kidding. Cochise knew it too, and that's why he packed a pistol everywhere he went. That's why he was never afraid to show anybody how cool he was.

For some strange reason I thought that that trip to The Other Side would be different. I figured we'd just pick the girls up, take them to the hotel and add them to the "Hit List." Not quite. Not with Cochise.

"L-up!" Cochise screamed out the driver side window at some cats standing on the front porch of the girls' house we were picking up. "L-up, niggas!"

L-up was Cochise's and everybody from his 'hood way of representing their block. It meant: "L-Town's runnin' shit, so you niggas better bow down." Everywhere we went, he screamed it. It didn't bother me, except for the fact it started a problem with someone every time.

I was from The Block. Since the only thing that separated Laclede Town from The Block was the Compton Bridge, our hoods cliqued up. People from my hood could go to Laclede Town and kick it with them and vice versa.

Me and Cochise mostly hung out all by ourselves most of the time. Hustling crack, packing heat and messing with girls.

"L-Town, killa," one of the cats said.

He was a small, puny-looking cat, but I could tell he was strapped with a pistol. All the puny-looking cats on the Other Side stayed strapped.

I don't know why we just didn't keep going when we saw them cats on the porch. If I was driving I would have. I was the type of person who would avoid a confrontation if I could. But Cochise? He was a different breed.

"Boy, shut up," said one of the girls as they came out the front door. She was talking to the cat running off at the mouth. "They're coming to pick us up." She turned to us.

"That's just my brother and his friend talkin' shit," she said, turning to her kin, "as usual."

"Cool," I said.

"Fuck dem niggas," Cochise said as he sped off, abandoning our get laid mission. "And fuck you hood rat bitches, too."

Damn, was I glad we didn't get into it with them cats. Since Cochise was driving, I would have been the one pulling the trigger. I had never shot anyone. Never had to. But, I know if it had come down to it, I would have. My partner might have started that static, but for some reason I didn't care. It was something about them Other Side cats that bothered me. I just didn't like them fools.

I mean, that was the first time in my life I felt like I wanted to kill someone. Just the fact that I knew them cats were punks playing hard and talking with their pistols made me feel that way. I really didn't need that shit on my conscience, though.

People had told me many stories about what it felt like to kill someone. Once, a dude told me he had nightmares for a week straight about all the people he had killed.

I couldn't imagine waking up in a cold sweat, holding onto the bathroom toilet, throwing up. Not at seventeen I couldn't. I didn't want to.

Although I had seen death before, it never bothered me. But, actually pulling the trigger? Damn, that had to be a messed up feeling.

At eighteen, my life was out of control. I was still in school (enrolled anyway), I still sold dope, smoked weed and gang-banged. I still planned on getting a scholarship to college. My grades were so bad from missing school so much that I had to go to junior college before I went to a big school. I was going, though.

The JUCO was only ten minutes from my house, so I was still going to be in The City.

The City was just as wild as it had ever been and so was I. Me and Cochise went on all kinds of capers in The City--carjacking, armed-robbery, drive-bys and any other crimes worth 25 years in the state penitentiary were committed.

Out of all the things I had done with Cochise, of all the crimes I had seen and committed, nothing affected me more than one event, late in the summer before my first semester of juco ball.

Like I said, it was late in the summer and damn near everybody in The City---This Side, The Other Side, The Best Side, The Least Side—and even The County for that matter---were creating havoc.

Everyday there was drive-by shootings, robberies, and stabbings. Everyday. For at least four straight weeks. Every single day.

Anyway, me and Cochise were chilling at a liquor store, right at the border of This Side and The Other side, getting some brew and blunt cigars for the weed. (The liquor store, The Spot, was a notorious trouble making breeding ground).

For the most part, the liquor store was not as prone to violence as some other places in The City, but it was something about the store that made it kind of a glorious spot to commit crimes.

I had seen a cat who I had got into some static with over a summer pick-up basketball game while I was in the store.

When he peeped me, I gave this look as if to say 'don't fuck with me'. And guess what? He didn't catch the evil-looking mean mug.

"Bitch azz nigga, what'z up," he screamed. "Talk dat shit you was talking on the playground, chump. 62euce, nigga!"

62euce happened to be a rival gang. When he screamed that, I knew it was on.

"62ookie killa'," I snapped back. (62ookie was a derogatory name for 62euce).

Cochise was in the car, so he had no idea I was about to get into some static. Shit, if he was in the store there wouldn't have been no time for name calling. Pistol-popping only.

"Hey," the liquor store owner screamed. "None of that stuff in here. Go home to ya' mamas or I'm calling the police."

"Yes ma'am," we both said, going separate directions.

I noticed he was leaving the store, so I followed him out the door. I'll be damned if I was going to let him get the drop on me first. The cat had made me so mad, that I had every intention of popping him when I got back to Cochise's ride.

"Nigga, start the car," I screamed at Cochise, reaching for the pistol. "I'm 'bout to blast that 62ookie over there."

"Over where?"

"That nigga over there."

I cocked the pistol.

"Whoa, whoa, whoa, Cass, get yo' ass in the car," Cochise ordered, struggling with me for the heat.

"What?"

"Get da' fuck in the car, nigga."

"Nigga, you trippin'," I protested. "I'm popping that nigga."

"Fuck dat chump, cuzz. Get yo' ass in the car."

Out off all the people in the world, 'Mr. 187 Takin' You to Heaven' himself was telling me to swallow my pride, and forget about popping the 62ookie. I couldn't believe what I was hearing. Cochise was usually down with popping anyone that messed with us.

"Aw'ight, bet," I said, glancing into the 62ookie's eyes. "Yo' ass is mine, chump. Next time, nigga. Next time."

The 62ookie couldn't have been strapped, because if he was he would have started popping. He must have been feeling good about his chances that day or something.

As disappointed and shocked as I was at Cochise, I'm glad he said what he said when he said it.

At the time I was really confused, but he explained to me why he told me to get in the car.

He said something to the extent of: "Cass Money, you have a chance to do somethin' with yo' life, cuzz, and I don't want too see you fuck it up. There's no reason for you to pop anybody. If you eva got static with anybody—ANY... BODY--, nigga, I'll pop dem foe ya'! I'm stuck in this madness. You. Shit, you gotta go to college, nigga, so I can sit back one day and see yo' ass on T.V. Fuck going to that JUCO. You need to get yo' ass out of The City and go somewhere peaceful. This ain't it, playboy."

MORE COLORS

I've always wondered what would happen if I got into a one-on-one confrontation with one of my enemies. (I guess you could call them my so-called enemies since I don't personally know the majority of them.) Well, one day—at what many in The City call "The Death Trap"—I got a chance to find out.

"The Death Trap", which I rarely even bother to go to, is a service station on The Other Side of The City. The only reason I was even there was to visit this hood-rat from The Other Side who lived nearby.

"What'z up, blood," said some 6-4 looking cat with long braids and red bandannas flanked on both hip pockets.

"I aint cha' motherfuckin' blood, cuzz," I said back with animosity. Even though I knew I was in dude's territory I wasn't about to back down. "Nigga, you'nt know me and you better keep like that."

Now I could tell dude knew I was about my work, but I also knew he wasn't going to back down in his own hood. Hell, the only reason we even exchange words was because I was wearing blue and gold and he figured I was a member of the Rollin' Sixties Crips, a LA based gang that had filtered into The City. His suspicion was right.

"Nigga, you'nt know *me*," he said, rebuffing my assertion of him and walking toward the entrance of the service station.

I still had to pump the gas I had just paid for and something told me this cat wasn't through set-tripping. Whistling and singing off and on to distract any onlookers, I smoothly reached in my stash spot and pulled out my shiny black 9mm. I jammed it in my waistband with every intention of using it if dude came out of the service station still talking shit.

My gas was through pumping at about the same time he came back out and I had a bad feeling about the situation. I figured he was strapped because he was jibber-jabbing so tough. I noticed him waving a car down that had turned onto the lot and my first instinct was to start blasting. I then thought about all the innocent people going about their daily routines, so I left the pistol in my waist.

"Blacca, Blacca, Blacca!" three shots rang out. "Damn, these fools is blastin' at me," I screamed to no one in particular, just alerting myself I had to go. As it turned out, the cats in the car was dude's partnas and they were trying to get on my head.

Being the survivor that I am, I started blasting back, using my car door as a shield. I kinda figured I was out-numbered, but I had to do something to keep from getting my cap peeled.

"I gotta get the fuck outta here," I continued my panic-induced speech amid hostile gunfire.

I continued to empty the twelve remaining bullets I had in the seventeen shot pistol as I jockeyed for a favorable escape route off the hotter than fish-grease service station lot. As I sped off the lot headed toward This Side the world seemed to be moving in slow motion. When you got three different cats with three different gats blastin' at yo' head, slow is definitely not the motion you want to be in.

"He getting' away, blood" one of the cats yelled out. "Get dat fool," he continued.

At that point in time I felt compelled to get out of dodge, but traffic on The Boulevard was stagnating any hopes I had of merging lanes. "You niggas can't touch me," I bellowed as I shot the last of my rounds at the Crown Vic the Bloods were in.

Ole' boy who I had the initial conflict with had jumped in the back seat of the whip the moment he let off the opening shots. I hoped he, at least, was hit, if not all them fools.

I continued southbound on The Boulevard several blocks away from the firing range before I noticed my stomach was feeling a lil' queasy. I figured all the excitement had me feeling butterflies. I looked down to see where I had dropped my pistol after getting down The Boulevard and noticed blood all over my lap. I instantly stopped the car and pulled over. I had seen the cats in the Crown Vic turn off once they realized they wasn't finna catch me.

My '81 Chevy Malibu had a 350 engine in it with a dual exhaust system and Holley Four-Barrel Carburetor. Them fools couldn't have caught me if they wanted to. I was still nervous about pulling over but I thought I was going to pass out at the wheel before I reached This Side. I got out to call my homie Chedda on a pay phone close to The Boulevard and MLK Drive.

"Chedda, cuzz, I'm hit," I yelled into the phone. "I'm hit."

"Cass, cuzz, where you at?" Chedda said, acting concerned. "Where the fuck you at?"

"I'm on The Boulevard, cuzz," I beckoned, feeling more nauseated by the second, "by the gas station on MLK."

"Who was you wit?" Chedda demanded. "What the fuck was you doing? Why you on The Other Side?"

"Cuzz, I was goin' to see this lil' rat."

"You talking 'bout that one lil' Snoop bitch we went to see the other day, cuzz?" Chedda wanted to know. "Man, I told you to stay away from that bitch."

"Look, cuzz, now ain't the time," I corrected Chedda, before passing out. "Meet me at The City Hos…"

STRADDLIN' THE FENCE (PART II)

"Damn, Schoolboy," my homie Chedda said to me as I stepped off the Amtrak train. "Dem fools got you liftin' all kinds of weights, huh?"

Chedda, who I had been practically brothers with since the 6th grade, was tall, lean, tough, cool, hip and angry. It seemed to me he was angry for no apparent reason, just angry. When a person has that trait, it is just a matter of time before someone feels the wrath of that person. With Chedda, they often did.

Chedda had agreed to pick me up from the train station because my mother couldn't find a ride. Although I had only been gone to college for one semester, he thought I looked different.

"Schoolboy, you look big as hell," Chedda continued. "You must be takin' dem 'roids, cause you ain't never been that big, cuzz."

"Naw, man. Just liftin' hard everyday and eating three squares, ya' know?" I replied, handing

Chedda one of the two travel bags I was carrying. "You been staying up on these streets, cuzz?"

"You know it, Schoolboy," he said flippantly. "Keepin' these marks off my head, ya' know, cuzz?"

"Yeah, I know," I said, guessing at what he meant."

"Get in the car, Schoolboy, I'ma holla at 'cha about it," Chedda said as we hopped in the car.

Now I could tell Chedda didn't really want to tell me about what dirty work he had done since I left, but because we were so close I figured he would eventually tell me.

"Schoolboy, you still about puttin' in work for the 'hood," Chedda asked me, much to my surprise.

"What kinda question is that cuzz, aint nothing changed?" Reaching into the bag I was carrying I continued, "I'm still about my work," I said, showing Chedda the chrome .380 I had brought back from school. "But I didn't come here for that," I said. "I came to see if I could find out where my son and his crazy ass mama at!"

It had been a few months since I had been back home and my son's mother had moved and not told me a thing about their new flats. I had sent my grandmother to her old crib in the Bluemeyer Housing Projects to see what had happened, but the house was boarded up.

To make matters worse, the phone had been disconnected and the new number was not listed. On top to that, none of her neighbors had a clue what had happened to her. They said she had just packed up and moved in the middle of the night.

I found it very hard to concentrate on school when I didn't have a clue of what happened to my child. I mean, he was really the only reason I was in college in the first place. Although I loved playing ball, that reason alone would not have been enough to keep me in school.

The fact that I had somebody to provide for, and take care of, and guide in life, made the decision to leave the gang life easier. Although it was hard at first, especially to my homie Chedda, the guys in the 'hood realized what was best for me and they supported me. After all, I never did say I was leaving the gang. I just wanted to get something positive out of life.

"Cuzz, I can't believe that gal just packed up with my son and bailed out like that." I continued, getting madder and madder at the thought of something as evil as what she had done. "I ain't done nothing bad to her, cuzz, ya' know?"

"Look here, Schoolboy," Chedda said, "that broad is gonna' need you before you need her and your son is gonna be aw'ight. I'm pretty sure she ain't gonna let nothin' bad happen to your baby. Cool? Now fire up some of that dank weed you brought back from college, Schoolboy."

For some reason Chedda had a point. Maybe she wouldn't let nothing happen to my baby, I thought.

"You know what, cuzz? You right. She ain't gonna let nothing' bad happen to him. Shit it's her baby too. Pass me the blunts so I can roll up this weed."

I had finally calmed down (the weed usually does that) and I was anxious to see my family. Even though we weren't a close family, I had always enjoyed them asking me about school and everything. Since I was the first one from my immediate family to go to college, it kind of gave me a sense of accomplishment to be able to say I'm enjoying it and having fun.

When Chedda and I finally hit the 'hood, we could tell right away something was wrong. I mean, police weren't new to being in the 'hood, but the ambulance and crime scene van was a surprise.

"Damn, Chedda," I screamed as we rushed upon the scene. "That looks like Lil' J-Spoon!"

J-Spoon, who was sixteen, was a full-fledged gang member. He had been since he was twelve.

To him, I was somewhat of a role model. He always told me he wanted to play sports because he used to hear everyone in the 'hood talk about how good I was playing ball. He told me the reason he joined the gang was because I was in it. I mean, everything I did, he copied it. I was hoping he would follow me on to college.

When he had got kicked out of school for fighting, I was the one who suggested he transfer to another school instead of dropping out. He dropped out. But all of that seemed minute when Chedda and I finally reached his lifeless body lying on the slab in a pool of blood.

"What da' fuck happen!" I screamed to no one in particular. "What da' fuck happen!"

In the midst of all the confusion and crying and screaming from what seemed like everybody in the 'hood, I spotted my grandmother.

"Grandma, what happen?"

"Oh, baby, I just got herre from work, so I don't know. When you get to town, baby?" she said.

"Grandma, who knows what happen," I asked fighting back the emotion I felt. "Who in da" fuck knows what happen!" I had never in life disrespected my grandmother, so she knew the pain I was feeling. Fighting back her own tears she said, "you need to go on in da' house and calm down. I'll send Cochise to find out what happen."

Chedda, who was as emotionless and heartless as anybody I've ever known, was also fighting back tears when he came into my grandmother's house.

"Dem Dukies did it," Chedda said, referring to one of our rival gangs, the Six-Deuce Crips

The frustration that I felt at that time of not knowing where my son was, coupled with the fact my little prodigy was dead at the tender age of sixteen, made me lose all sense of right and wrong. The only thing I felt was rage and revenge.

"We hoo-riding tonight, Schoolboy," Chedda said, letting me know our retaliation wasn't going to wait long to happen. "They take one of ours, we'll take ten of theirs."

Chedda, J-spoon's best homie Mouse and I had decided that we would ride for J-Spoon. After all, he was our little soldier. He was worthy of putting in work for, because he had put in much work for the 'hood.

I was still emotional when we first set out on our mission. Kill, Kill, Kill was all I could think of.

"Schoolboy, you're sure you wanna do this?" Chedda asked, needing reassurance about my role in the mission.

"Damn right!" I said, realizing I may be headed back into the negative element I was trying to escape from when I went off to college.

The closer we got to the Six-Deuce's set, the more apprehensive I got. J-Spoon would hoo-ride for me, I thought. He would. I knew he would. I also thought he would want me to go back to school, graduate and become a model citizen.

Before I left for school, I had told him I was going to come back to get him out of that madness. I had promised him I was not going to let him live a short life. We had discussed possibly everything imaginable and he promised me when I came for him he was coming back with me.

Now that he was gone, I didn't know how to react.

Would it be a disservice to him if I did not retaliate or would I be better off getting back on the train? I had promised to not let

Toriano Porter

anything happen to him. I wondered if I had let him down. Maybe if I would have called him and told him I was coming to town he wouldn't have been out in the streets. Maybe he would have been with Chedda when he picked me up and everything would have been alright. Who's to say 'what if', though?

All I knew was that I did not want to straddle the fence anymore. I didn't want be Schoolboy and Gangster. I had to make a decision and I did. Not only for J-Spoon or my son, but for my eternal happiness.

I made a decision about straddling the fence. I turned to Chedda and said, "cuzz, drop me off at the train station, I'm headed back to school, I don't need this no more. Get a lead on my son and find him and tell him Daddy coming to get him on my next break. Do that for me cuzz, would ya?"

FIVE DEEP (ME AND MY GANG)

December 22, 1994 is a date that will go down in history for me. No, I didn't win the lottery or lose my virginity or anything like that, but my life did flip a 360 degree script.

I was a lost soul; you know the sort of youngster that was raised to respect people, but had a tendency to hang with a fucked up crowd. I'm talking about a serious case of straddling the fence.

Well, in 1994 I had no love (or respect for that matter) for anyone, including my self. Hell, I didn't even give a care if I lived or died. I really didn't. I had my partners in crime, we had our straps and bud and we were armed and ready for an all out war. I was off into that gang-bang shit then, so you know I really wasn't giving a care. It was kind of crazy how I got to that point, but nevertheless, life wasn't worth a nickel to me.

My mind state in 1994 paled in contrast to my mind state in 1992, the year of high school graduation. In 1992 I was a three-sport star, great student, outspoken leader, and was nominated for homecoming king. I received a full football scholarship to Central Missouri State University, in 1992, and instead of going up, my life came crumbling down. Not all at once but slow and steady, like an outdoors man climbing a mountain and descending back down. The outdoors man is going to run into a few bumps along the way to the top, but once he reaches the top it is euphoria. And that's what happened to me.

When I signed that scholarship, I was on top of the mountain, feeling good, and thumping my chest. But, just like the mountain man, I had to come back down. It might sound strange, maybe somewhat ludicrous, but my fall was indeed slow and steady.

After graduation I was ready for college, (at least I thought I was ready), ready to attack it like I had attacked all of those running backs and receivers and quarterbacks on the football field. I played a little summer baseball to pass time, but lo and behold I started playing the dating game.

This girl, a sophomore at Eureka High, had a perplexing crush on me, throughout my senior year. We rode the same bus on our hour-and-a-half journey to school every morning. (Yes sir, I did say an hour and a half). Anyway, to cut the rambling tale short, I ran from her because she had a baby when she was only 13 years old. Actually, I was digging her but I wasn't the one to be buying milk and pampers for someone else's kid, if you know what I mean. Looking back on it, that really wasn't the reason, but it was a good enough excuse to keep me away from her.

Despite me ducking and dodging this girl all school year, we finally decided to chill together, about a month before college started. Excited and extremely hesitant (contradictions have the tendency to screw up ones life you know?) I asked the girl to attend my going away picnic with me. Sure enough, she said yes and asked me if she could bring her two-year old son with us. I obliged, but man, I sure did catch some flack when we arrived at the picnic.

My mother, grandmother and aunt all pulled me aside and berated me. Right then, right there. Called me stupid. Called me crazy. Hell, they even told me to take her home, right on the spot. The reason: my family had some wild notion I was going to make it to the NFL after college and they had some shallow thoughts about the girl. They claimed she was a scheming, manipulative, conniving, hood-rat that would destroy my whole life. Needles to say, we dated anyway for a whole year.

The year I spent with the girl was terrible. I left for college, got blamed for cheating (everyday), and even had a $989.00 long distance phone bill from calling the dingbat to assure her I had nothing hot on the side. That's not even the worse. She had my son, basically linking me with this devil-incarnate for the rest of my natural-born life. I'm not saying that having my son with me was the worst thing she did to me, (it was actually the best), I'm just saying, I was stuck.

Eventually, I got over the girl. I had to. I started dating her in 1992 and by 1993, she had dumped me. In addition, I had poor grades, a lost scholarship and no peace of mind. Not even the birth of my son on 4-22-93 could change the destructive path I was heading down.

By the time I hit the streets of St. Louis in the summer of '94, I was a full fledged gang-banger. Or at least I though I was.

Fresh from getting kicked out of Central, (I paid my way to go to school in 93-94 with student loans, and still didn't go to class), I was back in the city and the war was on. Not only the war between white and black, red and blue and good and evil, but the war between me and the demons that threatened to consume me.

I used to do dumb, suicidal things like walk through a rival gang's hood, with all my colors on. Shit, I even got on my bicycle once and rode 13 blocks with a .38 special tucked in my shorts. Like I said in 1994 the gang war was at an all time high and cats were emptying their clips at enemies on site. That's what I wanted. I wasn't brave enough to whack myself, so I figured if I traveled through an enemy's hood with my colors, they would take me out for me. It never happened (I guess they said, hey, that's a crazy motherfu…, we aint messing with him, he's probably got a grenade in his pocket, and is about to blow all of us away. Actually I was blessed, that's that creative twitch coming out of me.) I survived that summer of 1994, so I decided to go to a different college in St. Louis.

An almost impossible feat is to go to college in St. Louis, gang-bang, chase women, and use drugs. I couldn't pull it off. Something had to suffer and it was school in that case. The funny thing is that I didn't quit that school, they put me out. I deserved to get booted out on my ass, because I was fighting at school. But the two dudes I was fighting weren't even students at the school. Seems one of the dudes was mad at me because I called his girl a bitch, threw water in her face, and grabbed her by her collar. (I know that was a coward thing to do, but I really wasn't giving a fuck back then.) I felt she disrespected me and I reacted like a young, hotheaded confused person would; like a plum fool. The girl's boyfriend and her brother decided they wanted to protect her (I called them some "captain-save-a-hoe niggas", the slang used back then for dudes who were suckers for women), so they came to the school looking for me. I wasn't hard to find, the enrollment was only about 1,200 students. When they found me they tried to do bodily harm. Being the soldier that I am, I promptly whipped their asses. With the aid of a chair, I was a bad mama jamma that day. Too bad, I guess, because I spent 48 hours in jail and got kicked out of school. I wasn't tripping though, because I didn't want to go to college anymore anyway.

That incident led directly to my d-day. Like I told you, I had some partners and we were up to no good. When we found out the two dudes that I beat with the chair were going to be at this pre-Christmas Eve party we were going to, we possed up, five deep, at my stepsister's house in north St. Louis.

It was me, my homie Nose, my nigga from Central, Leon Moody, my basketball nigga from Central, Eric Simmons, and E-Double's partner Terry. E-Double, a standout basketball player on a Riverview Gardens High School squad that won the state championship in 1992, wasn't really off into that gangster shit like Nose, or as deep in it as Moody and me. He was gang-affiliated, though. I met him at Central when I was a freshman. As it turned out, his uncle was dating my mom, so we clicked.

Strange, but he left Central after the '92-'93 school year and when I transferred to the second college, Harris-Stowe, he was already there. We ended up skipping school almost everyday to go get us some chronic to blow. Everyday, we'd come back to school giggling, glossy-eyed and hungry to finish up our last couple of classes and go to basketball workouts or practice. Funny how people bond sometimes, ain't it?

Moody was my cat, I met him the first day of football practice in 1992 and it was on. Moody was two things at first that I didn't like; a wide receiver and a County boy. But he was serious about football and gang-banging and so was I.

He reminded me so much of my older brother BeanPole - tall, handsome, crazy, yet funny and loving - that we just clicked. Nose was like the wildest of us all. My best friend since the 6th grade, he was always there with me when the funk jumped. He plotted all the strategic plans for the night (except the one that called for us to wrap ourselves around a woman's front porch steps). So serious was he, he was the only one of the five that didn't get blowed out of his mind that night. He was as sober as the day was long.

Terry wasn't a banger at all. He was the designated driver for the night. He reminded me a lot of me before I started banging; young, confused, and overwhelmed.

After we all got into the car, I don't remember much. Oh, wait, I remember telling Terry to slow the fuck down, here comes a curve and telling E-Double, 'E, calm yo' boy down.' He hit the curve, a city curve mind you, going about 85 miles per hour and lost control of the wheel.

When I came back to consciousness, I was scared to death. I remember repeatedly telling my Aunt's boyfriend at the time to 'tell my son I love him. Tell me some I love him.' My knee and ankle hurt but I was the first one to get out of the hospital the next morning. Meanwhile, E-Double and Terry, the front seat passenger and the driver, were in comas, the direct result of flying halfway through the front windshield. Moody strained his knee and Nose broke his leg and arm. I visited every last one of those boys except Terry at the hospital. That was a painstaking experience.

Trying to describe the severity of these injuries would be a waste of time. All I can say is that we all lived and we all changed. Moody's change was the more impressive change for he gave up all the bull to spread the word of the Lord. He is really preaching and living through God. E-Double, one hell of a college basketball player never played another quarter of college basketball because of his injuries. He is working and is happily married with children. Terry moved to Milwaukee and is married. I believe he is back in St. Louis now.

Nose? I don't know what to say about him. He actually got worse and really stopped giving a fuck. Only recently, four years after the incident, has he shown any positive from that situation. He may enroll in college in January, if his GED score is accepted.

As for me, well I'm sitting here writing this and it's all good. I was at a low point in my life and it's almost like God reached out and touched me. Not so much on a religious kick, but he gave me the spiritual ability to love and respect again, and furthermore enjoy life on an everyday basis.

A PLACE WHERE HOOP DREAMS DARE TO LIVE

For some reason, I envisioned my first job after college being---actually I never gave much thought to what type of job I wanted , I just wanted to get my degree and get as far away from that damn school as possible.

But, I was thinking of something glorious like Sports Illustrated or USA Today or some sort of hot shot entertainment reporter in California. With a journalism degree, I was figuring I could make some major moves in the real world, you know? Get myself a nice car, a big house, a fat bank account and start a family.

The real world is a motherfucker, though, and I found that out quickly. Those six years I spent as an undergrad didn't prepare me to deal with job rejection after job rejection. Silly me. Who was I to think that those conspiring ass-holes would give a person with my background a job? The powers that be didn't seem to understand that a youngster at age 17 or 18 is not the same person at age 24 or 25.

Nobody was interested in hiring my services, so I started working as a master of the custodial arts at a local church. I couldn't believe I was working a 7 to 5 job for fucking peanuts.

Well, one day I was inside the sanctuary of the church, when I heard this voice.

"Cassius Clay Winston? Are you Cassius?" the voice said.

I knew I wasn't tripping because I hadn't smoked marijuana in months and that's really the only mind altering experience I've ever had.

"Cassius Clay Winston," the voice said again. I quickly turned around.

What was going on? I asked myself. Nobody was there, but I was seriously hearing voices. All of a sudden. BOOM! A sack of potatoes hit the ground. That's the last thing I remember. A big thud.

When the episode was over, the church's reverend, preacher, and gospel choir were standing, looking over me, singing, "Glory, Glory."

I don't know if I caught the Holy Ghost or not, but life changed that day.

"Cassius Clay Winston," another voice said shortly after the reverend dropped me off at my rinky-dink apartment on the city's Southside.

I remember looking around at the cubical - I mean apartment - and seeing nothing but white.

"Cassius Clay Winston," the voice said again. "If you seek him, he will find you."

What the he--I mean, I mean what in the name of Chr---I mean, what's going on? Find who? Who is he?

I had been attending services at the church I worked regularly on my off day (Sundays were my only off day) but the Holy Ghost had never hit me. I still didn't know what was up, but I decided to go with the flow.

"*Cass, Cass, God was looking out for us, man, I'm telling you.*"

"*Uh, yes he was.*"

"*Who got the gun, man, who got the gun?*"

"*Ion know, cuzz I think Chedda ditched it. Oh shit, Mook, my neck! My neck. My neck!*"

"*Cass, God was talking to us, man, he didn't want us to do that stupid shit, cuzz.*"

"*I know, cuzz. Doc, call my momma, man tell her I love her. Tell my lady I...*"

"*Cass? Cass? Cass? Wake up. Get up, Cuzz, God is with us. Get up!*"

He was not God, but it was God talking to me. Just like he had talked to my close friend Marty 'Mook' Mason seven years before, he was talking to me. But, in this instance, he was sending me to find Mook.

See, Mook was an ex-knuckle head turned religious man. We had developed a friendship when we were 18-year-old freshmen in college. As a matter of fact, we both played on the same intramural basketball team and had dreams of one day coaching some young-sters the way we wanted to play - fast and above the rim.

One day, we were going to get some payback on some guys who had tried to smash my head in at a party earlier that year. Me, Mook, my best friend Chedda and a couple of other knuckle heads had been planning our attack by getting high and pissy drunk all that fucking day. When it came time to do the do, we were so smashed, we crashed. Five high ass, drunk ass, wanna-be gangsters with one rusty half-silver, half-copper, half-working, six shot .22 caliber pistol. We never made it to our destination.

I don't remember much about the accident, but I do remember seeing my boy E-Double and his friend T-Lee hanging halfway out of the front windshield, courtesy of T-Lee's impaired driving. My other friend, Cheeda, had broken his leg but still managed to stuff the pistol deep into the console of the backseat while waiting on the paramedics. Me and Mook had gotten out of the car as soon as it flipped over, but we were both walking wounded. When we came to, I remember Mook telling me something about God being with us and to keep calm. Hell, I had never been unconscious before that, so I thought I was a goner.

Me and Mook used to talk every so often after the accident, but he changed schools. He also changed his life. He became fond of the Lord, and devoted his life to spreading the Lord's message. Mook never tried to pressure me into listening to his way of living, but he left the door open for me in case I ever wanted to find out about the Lord's word.

What was crazy about the whole thing with the voices was that I hadn't talked to Mook in years and out of the clear blue voices came to me telling me to go see him. To tell the truth, I was sort of ap-prehensive about tracking Mook down. I was worried that he would preach to me about not taking the same route in life that he took. I was afraid that he wouldn't approve of the way I was living.

After a week or so (I had quit my custodial arts job to following the voice) of researching possible ways to track Mook down, it all came to me. His Grandma used to live in the Central West End of the City so I would start from there. After a fifteen-minute drive to that part of town, I remembered his Grandma had moved to a retirement home on the outskirts of the County.

When I still couldn't locate her, I decided to call some alumni people at the college Mook had graduated from. After some nice talk, and some ass kissing, they gave me the whole low down on my man.

This guy was something. A degree in Religious Studies, the reverend of his own church and school, and president of Action Athletes, a non-profit athletic organization that allows athletes to stay in stride with the Lord.

There was only one problem, Mason Bible Reformatory School for Youth, was located some 200 miles from the City, tucked away in some small town called Great Haven. Seriously, I had never heard of this town, but I decided to pawn my treasured Rolex watch - it wasn't really a Rolex, but it had a Rolex face on it - for $80 and get a one way bus ticket to Great Haven.

After the eight-hour bus ride - does it really take eight hours to travel 200 miles? - I stepped off the bus to flag down a taxi. I'm thinking, I'll just take a cab to get to the school. Wasn't a cab in the whole town. If the truth is to be told, I was the only one to get off in Great Haven. After contemplating a series of moves, I decided to just walk, hoping to see someone to give me a ride to the school.

"Cassius Clay Winston, is that you?" a voice said from the left of me. This time, it wasn't in my mind.

"Holy shhh--- stuff," I said. "Mook, er, Reverend Mason, is that you?"

"Old friend, how are you? Heard you've been having some rough times."

"Whatcha mean?" I asked. "How did you know I---"

"Hey, word travels fast around these parts. Get in the church's van and let me show you your new office."

"My new what?" I asked.

"You new office," the reverend said. "You are the new coach of my basketball team. I have an opening for a guidance counselor and basketball coach and you are him.

"Are you serious?"

I don't know how long it took me and Mook to catch up on old times, but there were no regrets, no sorrows or hang ups about the past. He explained to me that he started the city of Great Haven - he actually called it God's city - and that his school was a reform school for teenage boys who had gotten into trouble and needed direction in their life.

"Good morning, gentlemen," the reverend said to each of the five school kids as they reached mandatory Morning Prayer service.

"This gentleman here is your new guidance counselor and basketball coach, Cassius Clay Winston, Coach Winston to you all."

"Rev, what we need a coach for," asked one of the boys, a lanky but still growing kid with two gold teeth in the front. "We don't even have a basketball team."

"The same reason you need those gold fronts out of your mouth," the reverend calmly shouted back. "It's God's will."

"Welcome, Coach Winston," said an odd-looking white kid, speech slowed and slurred. "Glad to have you be with us."

The whole room exploded with laughter. Even the reverend chuckled.

"That's going to be our center, Aleksander Petrovic," the reverend said. "He is from Yugoslavia. You'll have a chance to meet all of these guys one on one after breakfast. Let us pray."

Guidance Counselor/ Basketball coach? That's a step ahead of being called a janitor. I relished the opportunity. My first assignment was to organize a basketball practice schedule, a therapy session with each player and a list of possible high schools to play in basketball. Reverend Mason had told me God guided him to start a basketball team with those five kids he had. I couldn't argue with him I was there to do my job and follow his orders - or God's orders, whoever was giving them.

My first therapy session was with the kid with the gold teeth.

"Come on in, son," I said to the kid when he knocked on the door. "Start with your name and tell me your story."

"My name is Tamarr Roland and I'm 16. I'm from Houston, Texas and this is my story."

Seems this kid was a top-notch athlete back home, but had an older brother mixed up in the drug trade. Tamarr told me he averaged 26 points a game as a freshman on the varsity team at his high school in Texas. The reverend had given me the background on all the kids the night before, but I wanted to here what they thought of themselves.

"Man, I ain't 'bout to get into all that," Tamarr said when he was asked why he was in Great Haven. "Let's just say I was victim of circumstance."

The guy was a trip. He was engaging, yet evasive. Although he talked a great deal about the streets, he was reluctant to talk about his past.

"It's crazy down there in H-Town," he said. "Cats be robbing and shooting and not giving a care, so why should I. I just got caught up in some stupid stuff and paid the price."

"Reverend Mason told me you were the top-rated freshman in the country last year," I screamed. "And you fell off into some stupid stuff? What stupid stuff? "

"All I can say is I let my family down, I let myself down and I let the people in ward down. So the reason or the reasons I'm here makes no difference except I don't want to be here."

A self-professed playboy, I had asked Tamarr what he does for female company.

"To tell you the truth, the reverend don't allow us to talk to women except to study the bible with. I'm cool with that as long as I am here, but when I get back to the H-Town it's on."

"Well, why are you staying?" I asked.

"To get my act together," he replied.

When Tamarr left I remember thinking that he was wise beyond his years. He was also going to be my team captain.

The next guy I talked to was the foreign white guy, Aleksander. His father was a veteran of the Yugoslavian national army and Alek, 7- foot, 3- inches, was war-torn.

When his dad was killed in their country, Alek escaped with the aid of Reverend Mason's wife, Edith, a missionary.

The whole time we talked, which was brief because of the language barrier, Alek kept smiling. I didn't know if he was happy to be alive, happy to be out of his country or just plain happy, but he was happy.

I chalked it up to the fact he was playing basketball, learning about the Lord and life and didn't have to worry about the bullet ridden hardwood floors of his native country.

"Be cool, Coach," he said, smiling as he left.

I couldn't help myself, "you need to stay away from Tamarr, slang ain't English," I teased.

I hadn't seen Good Will Hunting in a long while, but my soon to be point guard, was him, I swear by it. His name was Will Fermino and his haircut and northern Boston accent made him look like an extra from the movie. This kid had it all. Two parents, nice home, a car at sixteen, and two older siblings who graduated from Ivy League schools.

"I'm noticing you don't look people in the eye much, Will, what's the problem?" I asked.

"The last time I looked someone in the eye they screwed me," he said matter-of-factly.

"What happened?"

"I knew this guy, crazy guy, best friend for my whole life. This cock-sucker steals a credit card and swears it's legit. Not on the Bible, but on our friendship. Anyways, we go on an all-out shopping spree, next thing I know twenty cops are waiting on me when I get home. My signature, my crime and that mother--- excuse my language, Lord help me, that sucker get off like a jack rabbit at a dog race."

"Nothing happened to him?" I asked bewildered.

"I ain't no snitch. Can't rat on my friends."

What a tough son of a gun were my thoughts when Will left.

The final two kids that I met with were DeMarcus Salee and John Carson, two former California Crips. These guys were inseparable and John had a habit of letting DeMarcus talk for him.

"John is a man of few words," Salee said. "He only trusts God now."

It turned out those two were trying to get some type of status within the gang when John a short, pudgy kid with big hands, was told to do a drive-by on some rivals. Salee objected, but John went ahead with the plan.

"That sissy of a gang leader was jealous over some cat knocking his woman up," Salee said in a half gangster, half kid voice. Salee had a bad habit of biting his fingernails and spitting them out; where ever, whenever. "But, the dude wasn't no banger. A dope dealer from LA, and John blasted on him. He wasn't even a dope dealer, though."

"What do you mean," I asked.

"The fool was undercover DEA," Salee said, mouth full of fingernails. "He didn't even get hit, but the hammer fell on my man John, ya' know?"

"Bums," John blurted out. "Just no-good, lousy burns. God bless their soul."

After that first session with those kids, it made me realize that youth can be corrupted very fast, but they can also be saved. Hell, it made me realize that lost adults can be saved, too.

Then all of a sudden, BOOM! What sounded like a hard knock against a table.

"Cassius, are you alright?" a voice said.

"Cassius, are you alright, son?" the voice said again.

"Yeah, yes sir, Reverend Williams," I managed, "just taking a small break."

A MIGHTY FINE INTRODUCTION

I love my girlfriend. My ex-girlfriend I should say. She dumped me about four months ago when she found out I had a three-month fling with a college freshman named Tiarra Brown.

Man, Tiarra was hot. I'm talking about she was just tall enough where her head could rest on my shoulders when we slowed danced. (We only slowed danced in private though because she was sort of my little secret, if you will.) She had those big brown eyes that you knew she had when she was about six months old; wide and cuddly. That's how she used to look at me when we danced too, like a cute little baby doll whose string was drawn. She had that cocoa brown skin and the softest, sweetest lips. Men are always talking about lips on women, but I'm telling you, her lips were soft, damp and tasted sweeter than a box of Russell Stover's holiday chocolates.

Anyhow, like I was saying, I really do love my ex-girlfriend. Now she has the beauty, the brains and the body that make guys label their girl's nines and tens. Plus she is super nice and respectful. DeDe--that's her name---is one of those slim and trim broads with those long legs that drive fools crazy. When she puts on heels, I swear we're at even keel. Her skin tone is tan brown like mine and she has the loveliest smile I've seen in all my years.

I can just picture the day we met. It was at the university's welcoming bar-b-que her freshmen year. I remember mentioning to a close friend of mine how I thought she was cute and had mega potential. My friend Mac kind of tooted his nose up and was like, 'naw, Cass, leave that fresh-meat alone.' I was smitten by her presence, though. Outdone to say the least. I knew I had to have her in my life.

Although I politely introduced myself to her and invited her to the football team's scrimmage later that evening, we didn't quite hit it off at first. Of course she used the 'I have a boyfriend' routine, but it was a shock to learn he was still a high-school student. Even though I respected her mind on that one, I knew their relationship would be a temporary arrangement. Can't no high-school kid touch me, I thought.

"That's fine, I'll just see you around campus then," I replied when she delivered the news of her commitment.

I don't know if my little gentleman speech worked or not but I do know DeDe became a little fond of me and made it a point to speak whenever we past by each other on campus. After a few months, that semester seemed to move along at a snail's pace and I was getting antsy for the Christmas break. Anyway, the football squad was doing a little holiday community service deal for the locals, so a couple of teammates and I were running around campus collecting can goods from the students in the dorms. Midway through our rounds, I bumped into DeDe and the first thought in my corrupted mind was "do you still have your little boyfriend?" Instead, I bellowed "hello, DeDe. Remember me?"

"How could I forget, I only speak to you every other time I see you," she playfully replied.

"Yeah, but do you remember my name?" I countered, placing the donated cans from DeDe's room into the hefty bag.

"How could I forget a name like Cassius Clay Winston," she asked. "Err, excuse me, Cass Money, Mr. football star."

I was astonished. "So you know about me, huh?" I said inquisitively.

"I've heard stories," she responded

I was in full throttle by then, though.

"Well, why don't you give me your number, so I can tell you if those stories are true or not."

"Like that?" she retorted.

"Like that," I deadpanned.

After a few more pleasantries, we exchanged phone numbers and I knew it was on. Man, hard to believe that was four years ago.

Speaking of four years, DeDe is on track to graduate in May, four years after she enrolled. Now, to me, that is an unbelievable accomplishment considering the things she had to go through during our often tumultuous relationship. See, that's why I say I love her because of all the soap-opera drama she's had to endure fooling around with me during her collegiate experience.

First it was my old friend Eriana, who I had met a year prior to meeting DeDe. Eriana and I had freaked each other, but we never had sex. I put DeDe abreast of the brief encounter, but she had a hard time believing Eriana and I didn't have sex. She really became suspicious when Eriana tried to fight her.

"DeDe, I didn't have sex with that girl," I told her after Eriana and a few of Eriana's friends became overtly obsessive with pummeling my baby. "She's just mad 'cause I won't leave you for her."

"Yeah right," was the only thing DeDe could muster out of her mouth.

Then there was Keena. DeDe told me Keena had been her best friend from seventh grade up until high school graduation. Kenna first went to college down south, but transferred to our school before the start of DeDe's sophomore year. She said she relocated closer to home because she missed DeDe too much. My guess she was wound too tight to fit in down south.

Keena and I started off cool. After all, she was my lady's best friend and they roomed together Keena's transfer year so I felt obligated to keep the peace. I mean, I had to show her love out of respect for DeDe, but I did think she was cool.

I don't know what happened with their friendship. It seemed so genuine and sincere that I never would have thought I would be the source of the tension. For whatever reason Keena didn't take to me and when DeDe refused to dump me, their relationship hit the skids. It actually came to the point that Keena and I had a verbal confrontation. It happened during an argument DeDe and I was having in their dorm room about some telephone numbers she had found in my Nautica Jeans' pocket.

"Look, DeDe, I done told you a thousand times, these numbers don't mean nothing," I protested upon learning DeDe's discontent. "People slide their numbers to me, I take them and throw them away. Honestly, I just forgot to throw those in the trash."

"Oh yeah," DeDe shot back, ripping the numbers in half. "Then let me help you with that."

I was peeved. Another heated argument followed and then boom, Keena spoke her piece.

"Get out!" Keena exploded. "I'm tired of you making my girl cry all the damn time. Get out of here and don't come back."

Naturally, I was stunned. Not only did Keena jump full-bore into our disagreement, she had the audacity to put her hands on me trying to escort me out the door. I held firm, looked at DeDe, looked back at Keena, then lost my composure.

"B****," I said aggressively, "don't you ever put your hands on me again." At that point, Keena was hysterical and DeDe was silenced. DeDe knew I had an ugly side, but I think she was disappointed that I would show it to her best friend.

"B****? B****?" Keena responded, literally bouncing off walls because I called her a name. "Oh, yeah? You get the hell out of here right now!" Keena picked up the phone. I thought maybe she was calling some of her campus henchmen, but she did me one better.

"Hello, Public Safety," Keena screamed into the phone, "we have a problem in room..." Anything she said after that is a blur because I was out of there quicker than greased lighting.

A couple of hours had past before DeDe and I spoke on the situation and by that time Keena had called public safety, her mother, father, brother, cousin and boyfriend. She even had the nerve to call my girl's parents. Boy did it take some damage control to keep DeDe's parents from throwing a hizzy-fit.

Keena was a nuisance to me after that encounter and became a hindrance on DeDe's and I love-nest. Suffice to say, they eventually fell out and when the smoke cleared DeDe was still in my world, down like four flat ones.

We made it through DeDe's junior year pretty much unscathed, but this year could be classified a sure-shot disaster.

Like I was saying earlier, the only reason DeDe's not my girl anymore is because of my fling with Tiarra. My purpose with Tiarra wasn't supposed to go down the way it did. Just so happened we had a communications class together last semester--Foundations of Broadcasting (she for the first time, I for the second). One day the professor assigned the class a group project, forcing us to partner up with someone we didn't know. Why did destiny pull me towards Tiarra? I damn near fell on my face trying to scrunch into the seat next to Tiarra's desk.

"I'on know you," I confidently noted, gazing into those amazing eyes. Like deja vu all over again, I introduced myself. "My name is Cassius Clay Winston and we're partners today."

She intently looked up from her notebook, and lovingly quipped "that's fine with me."

And thus my current predicament.

SHE'S GOT IT

The lady that lives next door to my aunt has got it. Pretty cocoa brown skin, nice slim shape, charisma, crib and car—I mean the total package. She has a couple of kids, but who doesn't these days?

I first peeped her a couple of months ago when I was home visiting for spring break. I usually posted at my aunt's house while I was home for the school breaks (Labor Day, Thanksgiving, Christmas, spring and summer) so I kept close tabs on all of her nice-looking neighbors. But, I had never seen this particular woman before. Fresh off the highway after driving three lonely, miserable hours, I noticed her and was instantly rejuvenated.

"Hi, how are you," I said confidently, unloading my bags from the '93 Chevy Lumina I had brought with the student loan I borrowed that semester. I thought I was being suave. Obviously she wasn't biting on what I was spitting because her reply was a snobbish "I don't know you."

Her response screwed with my emotions a little, but I stayed poised. I swiftly explained to her I was her next door neighbor's nephew home from college on spring break and I was just being cordial.

Know what she did? Yep, she slammed the door right in my face. With no words, remittance or hesitation. Just boom, goodbye! How cold-hearted that was, I thought.

"Auntie," I greeted my aunt as she crept outside to see that pretty young thing get her clown on with me, "who's your new neighbor?"

"Boy, that's Sheila," my aunt answered, adding, "she's a mean something and she's not studying your young butt, so leave well enough alone." Then she got clever. "Why are you here anyway?"

Man, I hadn't been home from school a good five minutes and people were already acting funkier than a dead dog. I kind of expected the step-child treatment from my aunt, but the neighbor was borderline rude.

"It's spring break," I informed my aunt, curious to find out the scoop on Sheila. "And it's on and poppin' already. Give me the vitals Auntie, give me the vitals."

Auntie looked puzzled "The what?" she quizzed.

"The vitals," I said, entering my aunt's apartment. "Where does she work, how many kids does she have? Where is her boyfriend? You know, the vitals?"

"Lil' boy please," Auntie screamed at me when I asked about the lady's info. "That women don't want no young, broke, do nothing brother with no job like you."

"Like me? Job?" I asked. "What is that suppose to mean? I play college ball, you know I can't have a job."

"No, you used to play college ball. Them days are over, hello!"

"I'm still on scholarship, though, so technically I still can't work."

"Any excuse is a good excuse," Auntie retorted. I was turning sour. "Damn Auntie, why you keep coming to me twisted and sideways, did I do something to you last time I was here or something?

I mean, all this heat and all I did was ask you about your funky acting neighbor. What gives?"

"What gives?" my aunt remarked, "what gives? I'll tell you what gives. You gives me something on the food you're going to be taking out my kid's mouths or gives me my damn door-key back."

"What?" I replied, trying to figure my aunt's angle.

"You heard me," she shouted. "You heard what I said."

Boy, I wasn't trying to blow up and go off on my aunt, but she was ego-tripping. I'm sitting there trying to get the scoop on the neighbor and she's sitting there stagnating progress. I had to ease the situation.

"Hey, straight up," I said to my aunt, "you need to hit some of this bud I got from my homeboy from K.C. 'cause you're tripping."

"Lil' boy you know I'on do no drugs in this house," Auntie scoffed, "at least not this part of this house. Let's go in the basement."

"See, now that's what I'm talking about," I rejoiced, "let's go in the basement, blow our brains back and talk about Miss Sheila, the future Mrs. Cassius Clay Winston."

"Lead the way," Auntie chimed in.

My Aunt's basement was a pretty cool duck-off spot for me. It was a typical South St. Louis basement: washer and dryer, a bunch of old stuff and makeshift living quarters for the downtrodden or hard pressed luck relative toward the back. I mean, I had my own flats back at school, but I was comfortable in her basement from time to time, especially late at night if you know what I mean?

"Where yo' kids at, Auntie," I started with the small talk, "at school still?"

"Why do you do that," Auntie moaned. I thought she was talking about the way I licked the cigar before splitting it down the middle with both thumbs.

"To empty the tobacco out, duh," I answered.

"No, fool," Auntie said "why do you ask questions and answer them all in the same breath?"

"I don't know," I countered. "It's a bad habit."

"Well, you shouldn't do that. It's a very annoying habit."

"Slow up, Auntie," I screamed, "let's not start that Cass Money bashing thing again. I thought we came down in the basement to relax and smoke some herb."

"Boy, you need rehab," Auntie bellowed out after watching me take a drag of the funny cigarette I had just rolled. "Lord please, bless my sister's second child would 'ya," she added, reaching for the blunt herself.

I couldn't do nothing but laugh at Auntie's outbursts. They were so full of venom they almost stung, but she always followed her evil words with something that let me knew everything was still cool between us.

"Not bad, nephew," Auntie exclaimed after her drag. "Not bad at all. Where is your friend from, Jamaica or Cuba somewhere?"

We were halfway through our session when I had another urge to ask about the next door neighbor.

"Okay," Auntie screamed, "you starting to get on my nerves asking me about somebody who ain't even studdin' you."

"Ain't studding who," I said, "me? You're wrong, Auntie, that lady loves me."

My aunt seemed astonished at my cockiness toward the situation.

"Pitiful," Auntie said. "Just plain pitiful."

"There you go doubting your lil' nephew's abilities again," I protested. "All I need is a good ten minutes. Two minutes to introduce myself, two minutes to make her laugh, two minutes to take her clothes off, two minutes to take my clothes off and two minutes to do our thing. Oh--and another two minutes to clean up the mess." I was getting louder. "12 minutes, Sheila, damn, give me 12 minutes."

"Boy, calm down," Auntie said, "that woman don't want you."

"How do you know," I asked. It had just dawned on me that Auntie was a little overprotective of this mystery neighbor and my curiosity started to settle in.

"Auntie," I said taking another drag of the marijuana blunt. "Ya'll ain't screwing each other are ya'll."

Auntie was stunned. "Boy, naw," she screamed. "I'll kick fire out your butt if you ever come at me like that again You herre me?."

"I was just saying, Auntie, you acting kinda jealous or nervous or something over there. What's wrong, Auntie? You high? Auntie, you high or something?"

"Quit playing so much," Auntie shouted back, "and I'll give you the scoop on Sheila."

After awhile Auntie proceeded to give me the low down on Sheila, and it was quite shocking to hear.

"Go upstairs and look outside," Auntie instructed me, "and look at the license plates on that green Toyota Camry out front. What do they say?"

"10-Step," I said, not understanding the relevance of the question. "What in the hell does 10-Step mean?

Auntie let me know that 12-Step was the drug rehab program Sheila had been on before she had moved next door. The word according to Auntie was that Sheila was a wild child from the Other Side of The City. In her late teens and early twenties she snorted coked, smoked weed and crack and snorted, sniffed and shot heroin, Auntie said.

"How old is she now?" I asked.

"About twenty-eight," Auntie answered.

I was somewhat surprised. "Twenty-eight?" I questioned. "That's all, twenty-eight?" I was getting more and more curious about this woman. "How long has she lived next door," I continued.

"She moved in around the first of the year," Auntie said.

"I thought them were some cats moving up in there?" I said, remembering the two dudes I had seen on my way back to school from the Christmas break.

"That was her brother and son," Auntie corrected.

Again, I was surprised. "Damn, her son looked kinda old," I said.

"She had him when she was twelve," Auntie said.

"Twelve," I said, perplexed. "How do you know all of that stuff is true, because that lady don't look like she used to be no dope fiend?"

Auntie flashed a cocked-eyed smile, reveling the gold tooth she had on the left upper side of her mouth "she told me."

"I thought you said she was mean?" I maintained.

"She is," Auntie said. "But I guess she wanted to talk so one day she knocked on the door and introduced herself." A mighty fine introduction, I thought.

"You lying." I said unconvinced.

"Seriously, boy," Auntie countered, "she came over and told me damn near her whole life story.

How she did drugs, stole things for a living, have sex for money, everything."

"Oh, so you're Oprah now?" I responded.

"No," Auntie casually said, "she just needed somebody to talk to and she knocked on the door. I never asked her one question."

I was still not convinced that lady, that beautiful lady, was a drug addict.

"Auntie," I said, "why you hatin' on me and my ballgame. If you don't think I can put her on my team then say that. Don't be coming out the wood works with all that non-sense."

"I'm just letting you know the truth to what you asked me," Auntie said matter-of-factly. "If you can't handle the truth, don't go asking for the truth. Like I said, Sheila used to be out there in those streets bad. She did some things and they have come full circle with her."

Again, the curiosity level was raised. "What'chu mean, Auntie?" I asked. "I ain't them little cookie cutters you popped out of your belly so quit talking to me like I'm in preschool."

Auntie, encouraged by my willingness to know more about Sheila, laid it on me. "Cass, Sheila has AIDS."

I was stunned. I was saddened and silenced. I couldn't figure it out at first, but it slowly came to me. Auntie wasn't hating on my game or trying to stop the unstoppable, she was just looking out for her lil' nephew. I wasn't quite prepared for the bomb she hit me with, but I was thankful Auntie really cared about me. She had funny ways of showing it, but I knew she cared.

"Um, um, um," I muttered after a prolonged silence. "Talk about blowing highs. I need me a drink or something. That pretty women next door has AIDS, huh, Auntie?" She nodded yes. "That's unbelievable," I finished up. "See, that's why I gave up baseball," I slyly joked as I helped my aunt up the stairs to her living room. "I'm always striking out."

THREE MONTH FLING
(YOU LOUSY SON OF A BITCH)

"Hey, baby girl, how you doing?"

"Fine."

"C'mon in here and let me take your coat off, I hafta tell you something."

"What's wrong, sweetie?"

"Nothing for real, but you might wanna sit down for this."

"Oh really?"

"Yes, really."

"Okaayyy, if you say so."

"Baby girl, you know I love you, right? Right?"

"So you say..."

"And you know I would do anything to keep you in my life, right?"

"Yes, I know."

"Well baby, I've got to let you know I ain't been right by you lately."

"Cassius, what are you babbling about?"

"Um...um...you remember that freshmen I had in class named Tiarra?"

"Vaguely. Why, what about her?"

"You know how we were in the same study group and we had to do our class project together?"

"Yeah, and your point is what?"

"Well, last semester we kinda got a little close."

"A little close? What does that mean, a little close?"

"You know, close, like talking on the phone, walking to class together kinda of close."

"Walking to class kinda close? Hell, fool, you don't even walk me to class. At least not anymore you don't. Go on..."

"Well, DeDe, we kinda had a um—a um—you know…a little something something going on on the side."

"Yeah right! That girl wouldn't give you the time of day. You and your little fantasies. Boy, where's my gift?"

"Naw, baby girl, I'm dead serious. We had a little thing going on."

"A little thing? You're serious?"

"Yes, I'm serious."

"Cassius, what are you talking about? Baby, you're scaring me."

"Baby girl, just let me explain."

"Yes, please do…do something, because I'm scared as hell you're about to tell me something I don't need to hear right now. It's my birthday for crying out loud."

"We were just study partners at first, youknowwhatI'msaying?"

"Yeah, yeah, yeah, I know all of that Cassius. Just tell me if you had sex with the girl."

"What?"

"Fool, you heard me. Did you fuck her or not?"

"Baby, we were just kicking it with each other at first, ya' know?"

"I don't care about all of that, Cassius, did you fuck her?"

"Yes. Yes I did."

"How could you! You…you…I can't believe you. No flowers. No cake. No card. No ice cream and damn sure no ring. Just 'happy 22nd birthday, DeDe. And Oh, by the way, I fucked some freshman.' I can't believe you would do something like this to me."

"Baby, I'm…"

"Sorry? If you dare fix your mouth to say sorry, I swear before a stack of bibles I'm going to kick your little scrawny ass. You have no right to say sorry. None. I'm sorry. I'm sorry I trusted you. I'm sorry I didn't listen to Sara and Jennifer. I'm sorry I didn't listen to my sister—she warned me about college men like you. Sorry? You're not sorry. I am."

"Baby listen."

"No. You listen. I can't believe you would throw three and a half years down the drain to have sex with some freshman. I should've known. They all said you were a little whore-monger, but no, my stupid ass believed you would change for me. Thank you for proving everybody right about your dog ass except me, you lousy son of a bitch. Thank you."

"Baby listen."

"What do you want me to listen to, Cassius? "How sorry you are? How you didn't mean for it to happen? How you regret it? Fuck that! I don't wanna here any of that!"

"Baby, would you just please let me talk?"

"Talk about what Cassius? Talk about how weak you are? How you like manipulating little freshmen girls? You can't pull a real woman with that wack ass macho game, so you go after little girls, you fucking freshmen groupie. You think you're a man? You ain't no man.

"Damn, baby listen! "There's more."

"More? More? How many more could there possibly be?"

"Not more woman, just more to the story."

"More to the story like what?"

"She um. I um. I mean, the girl is…"

"Oh my goodness, Cassius…just stop. I don't wanna hear anymore."

"She's…"

"Pregnant? You got her pregnant didn't you?

"Yes."

"I can't believe you would fucking do this to me, Cassius. Three and a half years and for what? On my birthday, Cassius! My birthday? I hate you, man. I really fucking hate you."

GENERAL ISAIAH

I can't possibly imagine enduring the forty weeks of struggle and uncertainty General Isaiah has just faced. Closed in, oblivious to the outside world, his only means of communication being his mother's sweet, sassy and soothing voice, echoing in his head.

The tossing, the turning, the upside-down pretzel-like twist consuming him during many confusing, sleepless nights. The hunger, the pain, the craving for some sort of relief. Man, way too many obstacles for anyone to overcome just to breathe fresh air.

Only two people really know the true facts that led to General Isaiah's capture. All that is known is one careless night of booze and drugs during battle will lead to major strategic mistakes.

Anyway it goes, the General had absolutely nothing at all to do with his current status, only abiding by the rules thrust upon him. There's no turning back now, though. Wayward on, son, wayward on.

Going along with the program, the General realized, rather instinctively, that in order to survive until he reached the outside world, he had to grasp for air on a limited oxygen supply and kick down the walls responsible for his confinement. The General played the part of soldier to the fullest, earning his much ballyhooed release from captivity.

Now, he's out. Look at him. Yep, he's a soldier alright, the epitome of a soldier; tall, long, dark and handsome not to mention the mental toughness to match.

The doctors and nurses are the first to greet the General upon his release. They're grabbing, pulling, and sticking all types of sharp, gleaming instruments in every nook and cranny from the General's ear-hole to ass-hole.

They're checking limbs, eyes and hell, those folks are even spanking the General, trying to get an emotional response from him.

Ah yeah, there it is. A thunderous cry that could have been heard within a five-mile radius if not for the plexiglass windows and closed corridors.

Welcome, General Isaiah. Wayward on, son. The world shall soon be your oyster.

APRIL'S NOBODY'S FOOL

April had just regained consciousness from the vicious right-handed back hand slap laid on her from her beau of three years, Papoose--Pap for short—when she realized, perhaps for the first time in that span, Pap wasn't the man of her dreams.

Of course, he was a charming son of a gun; well-framed, well spoken and naturally well-endowed. An educated, street-reared real estate developer in Suburban St. Louis, Pap was the ideal ladies man of the new era; sophisticated, educated, connected and paid.

Pap had--for a lack of a better term--whores all over The City of St. Louis and beyond. Northside accountants, Downtown loft-living advertising reps, Westside money go-getters, Central West End living radio personalities, Southside reared school teachers--not to mention the half dozen or so out of town acts. Pap had 'em all and April knew it.

She knew because she called Pap to task over his countless late-night disappearing acts. The 'I passed out on drugs at Mike Mike and 'nem crib' speech wasn't working anymore.

April had to do something, so she hired a private investigator who had just been relieved of his duties from the Cheater's program in Chicago.

He started his own P.I. firm in L.A. immediately after his dismissal. April's Left Coast living close friend of thirteen years, Maxine Tate, had drunkenly banged the P.I—Scientific LaPlure'--a couple of times out in Cali. It was Maxine who referred the overwrought, mixed descent sleuth.

"Girl you ever had some tropical fruit dick," Maxine would asked April during the countless weekly correspondence the two initiated. "Um, um delicious."

"Why did you hit me like that Papoose?" April asked, stumbling along the guard rail leading from the third level to the front door of the Miami Vice-type spread the two shared on the outskirts of the St. Louis City limits. It was a dream house for April, but just another piece of property to Pap, for he considered the place as valuable as the women in his life; beautiful, breathtaking, exciting, yet expendable.

Pap's love life was all a game to him. Business was business and he took his role as CEO of Papoose Urban Enterprises real seriously. The company was his life blood, his legacy. He had not a child. He loathed the responsibility of even having children, so he made sure he stayed strapped up with a condom on every woman he had ever slept with. Even April.

April wanted all of Pap's love. She had sucked it, swallowed it, jingled it—even took it through the back door, but had never had it raw. She couldn't help but feel inadequate. She thought Pap must be giving those other women the raw bone. Little did she know, he was not. Yeah, he was banging 'em, but he wasn't giving it to 'em raw.

"Bitch, you have the nerve to ask me a question like that," Papoose bitterly answered. "Bitch, I arta knock yo' motherfuckin' teeth out'cha mouth fa' speakin' such blasphemous talk. You know why you got knocked cross yo' motherfuckin' head….a motherfuckin' private investigator, bitch?"

"You crazy bastard," April screamed as she managed to steady her wobbling knees. "How dare you hit me like I'm some nigga off the street? How dare you….I'm calling the police….you going to jail tonight you big-headed, black fucker."

"I don't give a fuck about you calling no damn police, bitch," Papoose chided. "I got the motherfuckin' Chief on speed dial, you funky, in-bred bitch."

April reached for the cordless phone she had held in her hand when Papoose walked through the twin-glass-stained doors a few ticks earlier. Maxine, who was in town with the P.I., was on the other end from the Residence Inn Suite the P.I. had rented for his transplanted de facto office. He had all the best spy equipment available (hence his departure from Cheaters) and Maxine found that intriguing.

"Girl, I want him to fuck me with his infrared long-lense camera straddled between my tits,"

Maxine was saying to April before April was knocked silly. "April….April….oh my God…April."

"Put that motherfuckin' phone down April, before…."

"Before what, Papoose…you ain't shit….you big, black buff monkey, you ain't shit."

"Look, you retarded ass lil' girl, I'ma knock yo' damn ass out again if you don't put that phone down."

"Don't worry, Papoose, I ain't gonna call the police….I don't need to. I got yo' black ass, nigga, I got you. You don't think I got you, nigga, than try me. Maxine's got you. Scientific got you. We got you, you black ass ape. We got you with all them hoes. We got you with them two lil' white girls sniffing coke. We got you, nigga. We got you sliding them police them envelopes full of cash, we got you going into that strip club fucking them nasty stripper hoes---and paying them. That's prostitution, nigga. We got you. My P.I and his bodyguards are on their way here. The tapes are in the mail, nigga. We got you. Ha, ha, we got you."

By the time Papoose had regained consciousness from the beatdown he took from the P.I.'s bodyguard, he was in hand-cuffs. Not the police standard issued cuffs, but those cyber-space new styletype cuffs the P.I's favored.

The deal was simple. Cough up $200,000 in cash and let April walk and the tapes would remain sealed. Any resistance and the tapes surfaced along with domestic abuse charges and civil lawsuits. April knew Pap kept a money stash in a secret component of the house.

Pap thought April was blind—a fool—but she wasn't. She wasn't nobody's fool. She found out about the stash long before the P.I. and Maxine and the bodyguards came along to save the day.

April didn't need Pap's money, but she wanted him to pay. She would use the money to buy a condo in Mid-Town and pay the sleuth his fees. She would live off the salary she made as a top-notch administrative assistant at one of the city's largest business conglomerates.

"You funky bitch," was all Pap could muster as Maxine lead April from the laid-out pad the now-departed lovers had once shared in bliss. You funky, project ass bitch."

AGE AIN'T NOTHING BUT A NUMBER, RIGHT?

The heated exchange between my fiancé, Latrice, and I was much ado about nothing. Seems she couldn't understand the reason Coach Moore and the rest of the St. Louis Bulldogs semi-pro football team were all gung ho about our new quarterback prospect, Darryl Jackson.

Jackson was a do everything quarterback at Webster Groves High in Webster Groves, Missouri. Latrice, of Kansas City and still living there, had never heard of him, but I had. Jackson chose to attend the University of Missouri on a full football scholarship. Within days of his first practice at Mizzou, he abruptly left the team and un-enrolled from school. Some serious allegations had surfaced against him and he had to face the music.

"He did what?" Latrice harped when I mentioned Jackson had pleaded guilty of sexual misconduct after leaving Mizzou. "He had sex with an eight year old child? You've gotta be kidding me?"

"Yeah," I deadpanned, "seems he had sex with her off and on for at least five years." "How did he know the girl?" she asked, "were they neighbors or something?"

"Naw, nothing like that," I explained. "The guy was a part of the deseg program we got down herre and he and the lil' gal's big brotha was cool like that. They played football together and the dude used to spend the night ova therre all the time. One thing led to another, I guess. I know the shit went on for a minute, but as soon as the dude went away to college, the lil' gal told her parents about what was going on."

"Man, that's crazy," Latrice scoffed. "If that was my baby, I would want to ring that guy's neck. He shouldn't be allowed to play football ever again."

"See, that's the point," I said. "The judge sentenced dude to a hunnard and twenty days in jail and put him on probation for five years. Part of his probation stipulates that he can't play college football for the five years he on probation and he must either keep a job or be enrolled in school."

"That's where we come in," I continued. "The judge neva said nothin' 'bout the dude playing pro or semi-pro ball. We figure if we get him in herre for two years and he leads us to the championship, then hell, he may just get a chance to play pro ball somewhere."

"And you're cool with having a child molester on your team," Latrice admonished.

"He ain't no child molester," I corrected, "he's just a young guy who made a mistake. Now, I ain't saying what he did was right, but hell, when you thirteen and ain't getting none and you got some lil' gal who was probably as hot and horny as he was, let's just say the experimenting went too far."

"Tory," she screamed through the phone, "the boy had sex with a eight year old when he was thirteen and it didn't stop until he was, what, eighteen, nineteen? She wasn't even in high school when it stopped. That's a child molester."

"Well, technically, baby you right," I acknowledged, "and he does have to register as a sex offender, but does that mean he shouldn't be allowed to play the game he was born to play."

"Hell no!" she protested. "Especially, if he is going to get paid."

"Well, we don't get paid," I explained, which I don't know why because if we had gotten paid

Latrice wouldn't still be asking me about the ring she didn't have to make our engagement official.

"But, if the Arena League comes or the Canadian League come calling for him, then it's all good. America is all about second chances, right?"

"I don't care what you say," she expounded, "he should never be allowed to play for pay. Never. Make him get a real job and contribute to society."

"I'm saying, Latrice, the dude already gotta pay the lil' gal for any medical or psychological bills she gets from here on out, so I'm pretty sure she wants him to make it to the League too."

"Oh my God," she pressed on, "how can you say something like that? If that's how you feel, I may have to re-evaluate this situation. There is no way I can condone you condoning that type of behavior."

Within seconds, she had hung up and refused to answer my calls the rest of the night.

WITH OR WITHOUT THE RING

"Oh, Tory, I would love to marry you," the mother of my six year old son, Latrice, said to me when I asked her the proverbial question. Of course, I wasn't meaning exactly then, but I knew I wanted her to be in my life forever. "Where's the ring?"

We were dining out for Latrice and our son General's fifth birthday, which fell on February 2nd and 3rd respectively. Geno, as we call him, was busy scarfing down the chicken strip plate his mom had ordered for him. Latrice was nibbling on a side house salad (something about a low carb, or high carb or South Beach or something diet) and I munched on a steak and chicken plate.

Eschewing the normal down on one knee approach for something a little less, shall I say, embarrassing, I laid it on thick about being in love and wanting a traditional family for our child to be reared in. The only problem was I didn't have a job, car or savings to start the family off the right way and that made me reluctant to commit to Latrice. I forged on.

"Listen, baby," I said cunningly, "I know you want a ring. Hell, you need a ring to make this thing official, but work with me for a minute."

"What's a minute, Tory?" Latrice wondered aloud, pushing the side salad away from her proximity. I'm not getting any younger here and I want another baby."

"Baby, I don't know," I protested, "you know I'm going through some tough times right now. There's nothing more important to me in life than to have you and Geno with my last name. You guys are the air I breath. I love you both. I need to find a job. Until then, baby, just take these words and know you'll get that ring you've always wanted later."

Latrice, a medium height, brown skinned beauty of a woman, wasn't amused, yet she understood my situation.

"Tory, you know I love you," she explained. "I love you sooooo much. But how in God's name, do you even attempt to ask me to marry you and you don't even have a ring. I mean, really, Tory. I've put up with your football dreams, your rap dreams, your writing dreams. All I dream about is a family and having a husband responsible enough to provide for that family. Right now, I'm doing this by myself and it's extremely hard for me."

Geno, who by that time was working over the banana flavored desert cake the waitress was generous enough to provide on the house, was eavesdropping. The six year old baby genius (the kid attends an elementary school that teaches the entire curriculum in French) added his two cents.

"Mommy," Geno said, "what's wrong? Why are you crying?"

"Oh, Geno," Latrice replied, "Mommy's just happy right now."

"Then why are you crying, Mommy?" Geno deadpanned. "People don't cry when they're happy, Mommy. Do they Dad?"

"No son," I replied, "they're not supposed to."

"Excuse me," Latrice said, rising up from the brown marble table that held our dinner. "I have to go use the restroom."

Latrice was gone for a short while, but not long enough to cause concern. I knew the chances of her saying yes to marriage without a ring were slim, but I had to try. I love the girl and I want to marry her, it's just my financial situation is dire and I can't afford a ring. She has definitely gone beyond the call of duty in supporting my dreams and career goals and I know I must make it right. Again, I forged on.

"Geno," I said, "when your Mom gets back, I want you to kiss her and say that's from my Dad. See how she responds, ok?"

"OK, Dad," Geno said, "I will."

On cue, Geno delivered the kiss and message, while I looked on. The twinkle in Latrice's eyes made me feel comfortable that we would somehow make it work.

"Oh, Geno," Latrice gushed, "Tory!!! You are the sweetest. I love you, baby. Let's go home and talk about this some more. Maybe you can get me a ring when you sign your first book deal."

BACKGROUND CHECK

I knew, subconsciously perhaps, that my ladies' man reputation may have preceded me when Tracie didn't return the last of my five phone calls. I mean, just two nights earlier we'd had our first date. It was great. We met promptly, ate well and drank mercifully at O'Charley's Restaurant, all the while conversing about life situations.

After dinner, we went back to her non-descript one bedroom apartment. Over a post-dinner celebratory funny cigar, we discussed our professional lives, eventually leading to our talk about college life. She mentioned she had attended my alma mater for two years before transferring, which coincided with my last year there.

"Are you serious?" I asked her when she informed me of her two year stint at Central Missouri State University in Warrensburg, Missouri. "You went to CMSU?"

"Yes," she replied, "but I had to leave. I was tired of the people up there always in my business."

We couldn't remember each other from campus, but we both knew some of the same people.

After awhile, it became apparent that we may have known each other but were unaware of each other's core existence.

After going out dancing together for a few hours that night, Tracie mentioned she would try to get the inside scoop on me from some of her old CMSU friends before our next date. I didn't think much of her sleuth work until the second date never materialized.

She must have gotten a bad word.

THE EVENING WHIRL

"You know, Toronto," Detective Mack "Stone Cold" Stone said, struggling to pronounce the young reporter's given name yet again.

The reporter, Toriano "Don't Call Me Tito" Jackson, was a first year scribe for America's number one crime fighting publication, *The St. Louis Metro Evening Whirl.*

The Whirl, had recruited Jackson after *The County Journal* canned Jackson for insubordination. Jackson had tried to land a gig with *The City Journal,* but to no avail. Those publications were owned by the same enterprise, Pendulum Press Inc.

The Whirl's publisher, Avery A. Anderson, had met the young Jackson at a media function and kept tabs on Jackson's work periodically. When Avery learned of Jackson's demise, he pounced on the opportunity to hire a young, seasoned journalist for his tabloid like, scandal laden paper.

"I've been thinking about something," the detective said, continuing a conversation Jackson had no idea what about. Stone, who was initially against Jackson's three times a week ride along position had warmed to the kid after a while. Stone's beef was having a nosey ass reporter trailing him, asking him questions about how he gathered evidence, suspects, witnesses and the like.

He didn't want the scribe to relay to readers some of the tactics veteran homicide sleuths used to collar their criminals. Stone just wanted to finish the year out and retire a thirty-year vet of the St. Louis Police Department. He didn't want to hear anything about Sunshine Law violations, PR campaigns, or private settlements.

The brute, not so meticulous, crime fighter labeled the ride along plan 'reality TV, in print'.

"We've come a long way, me and you kid, wouldn't you say?"

"Yeah," Jackson said, joking, "but you're still screwing up my name, Sir. It's Toriano, not Toronto. Toronto is a city in Canada, you know?"

"That's right," the balding, husky built Stone said, chiding Jackson about Jackson's mother's choice of tag for her second born son, "Tito Jackson. Can't believe ya' momma named you after Tito Jackson. That's some funny stuff there boy."

"Ha, ha funny." Jackson said, staring out of the passenger side window of Stone's Chevy Impala. "Real bleeping funny, Sir."

"Oh my bad," Stone said navigating a right turn onto Grand Blvd. from North Florissant Avenue. They were headed to the Walnut Park area of the city and Stone wanted to hop on Interstate 70. "Ya' aunt named you. I forgot. She's funny. I wanna meet her some time. What's her name again?"

Jackson had become fond of Stone's ribbing during his three month stint and he enjoyed Stone's acceptance. He felt Stone had validated his sense of a journalist somewhat.

After initially closing and pulling rank on the scribe, Stone eventually opened up to Jackson, showing his ins, outs, tidbits and scoops of a decorated detective. Stone's only request of Jackson was for Jackson to give him co-producer credit on any film project or book deal Jackson put together after his ride along plan. "You know, Hollywood type stuff," Stone would say.

"Theresa Bell," Jackson said, reminding Stone for the umpteenth time of Jackson's mother's close friend's name.

"That's right," Stone said, still wise cracking, "Theresa Bell. With a name like that, you need to hook us up nephew. She probably know how to love a big ole' teddy bear like me. Huh? Is she married?"

"No," Jackson said, ignoring Stone's overture for Jackson to call his aunt and make some magic happen. "My auntie does not... I repeat Sir, does not... date police officers, alright? So no, I won't call her."

Stone was livid. He imprudently pulled the Impala to the side of Grand Blvd. near the Northside water tower. Jackson was shook.

"Let me tell ya' something, you little cocksucker," Stone said, screaming at Jackson with the bellow of a mad man while grabbing the unsuspecting scribe by the collar of his $19.99 Polo shirt he had gotten from his favorite shopping hunt, Burlington Coat Factory on South Kingshighway Blvd. "I will break your freaking ass in two, if you ever call me a freaking police officer ever again, you understand me? You disrespectful pencil neck geek."

"Yes sir," Jackson said, pleading for Stone to let his neck go. "I can't breathe right now, sir."

Stone definitely had some serious meat hooks. Jackson was surprised by the vigor in which Stone reacted, but he had seen it plenty of times before. Only he had a standing oath with Stone that he would never divulge the detective was violated criminal suspects' civil rights when he applied the meat hooks to them. Jackson immediately apologized.

"Detective Mack Stone," Jackson said. "Stone Cold. Bad Ass Super Cop… oops I mean Detective, sir. Bad Ass Super Detective. 'Always gets his man. By any means necessary, collar the bad guy'. My bad sir, it'll never happen again, sir."

"You're pushing it Toronto," Stone said, less peeved than thirty seconds before, but still steaming. "Let it be, and let me get back to what I was saying."

"Which was?" Jackson said smoothing out the collar of his now frazzled shirt. "Like I was saying," Stone said, darting back into traffic headed toward his destination, "we've come a long way and I feel I can tell you what I'm about to tell you and it won't end up on the front page of The Whirl."

"Which is?" Jackson said, noticing a pretty lady pull up along side of them. She was in a late model white Chevy Impala, similar to Stone's department issued vehicle. Jackson waved at her. The sand blond dyed hair woman wore her hair in a little twist. She waved back.

"Hey!" Stone said, "Look at me, listen to me, this is some serious stuff I'm a bout to unload on you, and I need you to put this under our oath."

"O.K.," Jackson said. "Chill, you're missing the highway ramp."

"I've got this wheel," Stone said, swerving onto I-70 the only way he could without hitting or hurting someone. "Son I've been doing this for thirty some years. You don't think I know to climb the highway doing a little bit of speed?" C'mon, Toronto, you've rode with me enough to know that I aint gonna hurt cha'."

"Right," Jackson said, doing something he should have done earlier—buckled up his seat belt. "I forgot."

Darnell "Da Dart" Davis was not what you call a career criminal. He had picked up the criminal lifestyle after loosing his basketball scholarship at University of Illinois—Chicago. He had gotten caught selling marijuana on campus and expelled from school.

Instead of coming back home to St. Louis, he posted up in Chicago for a few years, graduating from selling weed to heroin, to crack and cocaine. He made dough, but it wasn't the serious dough he needed to sustain his lifestyle, so he decided to head back to St. Louis to set up a distributing network with some old neighborhood associates.

The associates, a band of North City thugs labeling themselves as the C.R.E.A.M. T.E.A.M., for their self perceived penchant for getting fast cash, were guys who grew up in the same Walnut Park neighborhood as Davis. They had always admired Davis for his ball playing skills and ability to steer clear of the negative elements that surrounded the crew. They represented for Davis at all of Davis' games at the local high school and threw him a huge going away bash, the week before he left for UIC. He never forgot the love. When he came home Chicago connected, he had to return the love to the C.R.EA.M. T.E.A.M., specifically, Arturo "Young Gotti" Young, the de facto leader of the crew.

Young and Davis had balled together at the high school, but Young dropped out as a sophomore to hit the grind. The crack epidemic hit and Young felt like he had to get his while he could, because basketball wasn't a guarantee. He needed bread and he needed it then. He hit the streets and hit them hard, creating the C.R.EA. M. T.E.A.M with Barry "Guerilla Black " Thomas, now deceased.

Young and Thomas recruited a couple of middle school kids and went to work. The middle schoolers, Tony "Tech" Thompson and Ralphie "Da Rat" Wallace hustled the dope and Young and Thomas doled the dough. They broke the youngsters off enough bread to keep the youngsters clean and reinvested the rest of the profits.

True, Young and Thomas stayed clean too, but they bought buildings, old warehouses, junk cars and the like and legally created an enterprise, CT Associates.

CTA profited from selling buildings for double of what they paid to renting out warehouses to host raves and art exhibitions. Whatever junk cars they didn't spruce and tighten for themselves, they sold. Thomas was killed two months before Davis arrived back home and the crew was still reeling. Thomas had had the connect and the connect may have had something to do with Thomas' murder.

CT members had never known who the connect was because Thomas was sworn to secrecy by the connect. Death would be the sanction if Thomas ever divulged the connect. He never did. Not even to his right hand man, "Young Gotti."

Young respected Thomas' position, but it tore him up after Thomas' death. He didn't know who to hurt, so he swallowed Thomas' death with a bitter pill. Davis was a source of hope when he eventually touched down. Although CTA was thriving, the fast money allure still ran through Young's veins as well as the other CT members.

Davis' Chicago connect put CT back on, with Young taking over the leadership and head decision making role. Young wanted Davis to sit back and learn the streets of St. Louis again. CT moved differently than "those Chicago cats," Young would say. He wanted to show Davis how their crew moved. They agreed to split the profits evenly and disbursed the proceeds evenly among their stable of workers, giving "Tech" and "Rat Boy" lead crew status and extra dough.

For a nice three-year stretch Davis did well with CT. In fact, the whole crew did well until conspiracy and money laundering indictments came raining down. The whole crew stood firm. At least until Davis cracked and decided to turn Government witness. He brought the whole crew down, in exchange for a three year bid at a federal joint in Illinois.

"I think the feds killed Davis," Stone said, exiting I-70 at West Florissant Avenue, headed east. "I really do."

"Are you serious, sir," Jackson said in utter surprise. "Why would the feds kill Davis?"

"Think about it for a minute," Stone said. "Everybody associated with the C.R.E.A.M. T.E.A.M. knows that Davis was the Government's star witness, right?"

"Right," Jackson said, making mental notes for a possible expose The Whirl had been known for.

"Who freaking kills a government star witness?" Stone said, expanding on his conspiracy theory. "Not CT or anyone close to 'em. They have enough problems than to send someone after Davis. Besides they are all in the bin and you know mail and calls are monitored like a son of a gun, right?"

"Right?"

"So here's the deal," Stone said. "Davis' ole' lady told me over the phone that he was trying to get out of dodge because he wasn't suppose to come back to the neighborhood. The cocksucka had a deal with the feds that he wouldn't tell NOBODY where he was headed and what he had to do for them. He told her he wasn't supposed to see her or the kid, but the cocksucka had to see his lady and kid, right?"

"Right."

"Don't nobody mess with the feds, Toronto, " Stone said, arriving at his destination, Davis' wife Keisha "Da Sneek" Davis' home on West Florissant Avenue and Queens street. " Nobody. They say left, you go left. They say jump you say how high. You do what you're told or you're done, bottom line. The feds offed this kid and I'm going to crack it open. Cocksuckas got us running around like lost chickens with our heads cut off and they're right up under our noses talking about undisclosed award money for information. They're not naming a price because there is no price. They have no witnesses. I'm going to find out what Sneek Davis knows about her beau getting wiped out eleven hours after he gets out the bin. Who moves that fast?"

"The Feds!" Stone and Jackson said in unison.

****

Darnell knew he wasn't suppose to visit his girlfriend of seven years, Keisha, after he served his bid. But he couldn't imagine relocating without seeing her and their son, Elijah again. The pair was never allowed to visit Darnell while he did his bid. Letters and phones were what the couple was reduced to.

Darnell only agreed with the deal because he didn't want to spend twenty-five years in the joint like Young, "RatBoy" and "Tech." He could manage three years. But, twenty-five? No way.

Although he brought the whole crew down, his name was mud on the streets of Walnut Park. Even rival dealers had him on the hit list.

The feds warned him about going back to the old neighborhood, but Darnell couldn't stand being holed up at the Airport Hilton waiting on his flight some twelve hours after he reached the airport from Illinois. He had to see Keisha and the baby.

That vigor may have cost him his life. No less than twenty seconds after Keisha kissed Darnell goodbye she heard a voice and then shots. More than three. More than four. She didn't know how many. No shell casings were found. Darnell died from the two gunshots to the side of the temple. His body was riddled with a shot to the torso, chest, and upper right thigh. The coroner pronounced him dead on the scene.

"Excuse me detective," Davis' now widow Keisha said, sobbing after Stone's opening line of questioning. "But this is all too much for me right now. I didn't even know he was coming here. He shows up, talking about this, that and the other. Stuff like, 'what would you do if I died tonight? Would you cry? Would you kill for me? Would you plan my burial? All this stuff about death. That's why I stopped writing him and accepting his calls. All he talked about was death, like…like…like he knew he was going to die."

"Listen Sneek," Stone said, making amends with Davis, "if I may call you Sneek?"

It's ok my friends call me Sneek, the widow said.

"That's good," the Detective said, "consider me a friend. Who did Darnell say he thought would kill him?"

"The C.R.E.A.M. T.E.A.M.," Keisha said. "The em'effing C.R.E.A.M. T.E.A.M."

"Didn't he know that he put the whole team behind bars?" Stone said, questioning the Davis' paranoia. "They wouldn't dare send somebody at him, you know?"

"I tried telling him that he was a government witness and he was as protected as anybody with a badge or a gun," Keisha said. "But he kept saying 'ef the feds, they probably gon' be the one to pay the C.R.E.A.M. T.E.A.M. to whack me.' This is all just so... so... just bad."

"Did he say why he felt like that," Stone said mentally taking notes of Keisha's response, demeanor and posture. "You know why he felt the feds would pay the homies to whack him?"

"That's what I'm saying detective," Keisha said, "those type of statements are what had me stop talking to Darnell. I was scared... and now I'm mad. I'm mad 'cause he came herre, gave me hope errything was going to work out and we would be together soon. I didn't believe him. He's gone now and I didn't tell him I loved him the whole time he was herre. I was just so mad at him. I'm mad still, but I'm mad that he's gone and I didn't tell him how I felt. He shouldn't have came herre."

"Why do you say that?" Stone said, "he shouldn't have came here?"

"Errybody ova herre know he ratted out the whole C.R.E.A.M. T.E.A.M. Hell errybody in St. Louis know he got errybody from the T.E.A.M. locked up, that's no secret. But he knew he wasn't supposed to come herre 'cause of the Feds. He told me, they told him that he couldn't see us before he caught his flight to wherever they were relocating him to."

"Where was he going?" Stone said.

"He couldn't tell me. He just said he had a few hours before he boarded a private jet to his location, and that was that. He didn't even know where they had him going."

"Did he say what they were going to have him doing?" Stone said, pondering the feds motivation to keep Davis away from his family.

"He said they hadn't told him exactly what they were gonna do," Keisha said, "but he kept sayin' a couple of inmates in Illinois were sayin' how they use federal witnesses to infiltrate drug rings, when they relocate them. He said he wasn't selling no drugs no more. Not for the Feds, not even for his family, and that meant a lot to me, but I was still mad."

"Why were you still mad at him, Sneek," Stone said.

"Cause he turned federal," Keisha plainly said, "and errybody around herre know I'm his wife and wouldn't nobody talk to me. I lost all the friends I had. I lost my kids father, my friends, and my family. My mother is too scared to even visit over herre. We're so alone right now."

"Who knew he was coming home," the detective said. "Who did you tell?"

"Nobody," Keisha said, insisting she wasn't aware of Davis' homecoming either. "He just showed up."

"He knocked on the front door?"

"No," Keisha said, " actually came knockin' in the side sun porch over there. Scarred me halfway to death."

"So, why did he leave out of the front door?"

"That…" Keisha said, still emotionally distraught, "… I don't know. I hadn't even thought about that."

"You mind," Stone said, getting up out of the sofa Keisha had offered for his convenience.

He wanted to see the sun porch and the side door. "C'mon kid, let's go. Mrs. Davis has had enough trauma for a day. Sneek, thank you for your time. I'm sorry about your loss. I'm confident we're going to get our man, or men on this. Here's my card. Please use it, alright? Any questions, anytime use it. It's my private line."

"Kid, I'm telling you, the Feds offed Davis," Stone said driving south on the one way Queens Street, away from Davis' home. "That housc is under surveillance. Bugs everywhere. Guarantee you. Watch this."

Stone had pulled over on Queens, just a short distance from Davis' home. He sat back and waited patiently. Jackson, the scribe, was perplexed.

"Sir," Jackson said, "for technical purposes, what are you doing?"

"I'm doing what good detectives do," Stone said, "playing a hunch." Within seconds, from their perch a block or so from the Davis', Stone saw a new model expedition pull close to the home they had just left minutes prior. Two men, one tall, brown skinned with a short crop of hair, the other a shade darker, a shade taller and distinct wave pattern of hair. The blue light weight jackets the pair sported read: FBI.

"Those cocksukas offed Davis." Stone said, darting the Impala out into traffic with usual abandonment. "He didn't play their game with 'em and they offed him. Guarantee you. I'm going to crack this case wide open kid let's go back."

The federal agents at the Davis' home, Agent Caldwell "Gaffle 'Em Up" Jones and Agent Ryan "Guilt Free" Reynolds, were two former STLPD detectives who were now employed at the FBI's Eastern District of Missouri office in downtown St. Louis. Stone was never fond of the pair, as he considered them hotshots upstarts with federal aspirations. Stone felt, nothing was wrong with the pair's ambitions, he just didn't like the manner in which they went about attaining their goal.

"Federal cocksuckas," Stone would say, "those cocksuckas are some Federal brownnosers." Needless to say, the pair was surprised by Stone's re-entry.

"Stone Cold," said Agent Jones the taller of the two. "Your time is up for the day Mack, break wide, we got this."

"Listen cocksuckas," Stone said, "I'm here to question a witness to a homicide, and I'm not about to let you federal flunkies badger her about what she may or may not know."

"Well, Stone," Agent Reynolds said, adding what two cents he felt worthy of putting into the conversation. "Your homicide case, is now a Federal case, so goodbye... you're the weakest link."

"But, Chief," Stone said to STLPD police chief Roy "The Terrible" Taylor, shortly after Chief Taylor informed Stone of Stone's removal from the Davis case. "I'm telling you that the Feds offed Davis."

"Leave it alone, Mack," the Chief said, warning Stone of the consequences of such allegations without substantial evidence. "It's a Federal witness in a Federal drug case, there's nothing you or I can do. It's theirs from here on out. Leave it alone Mack, and hold those conspiracy theories a little more closely guarded. You do want to enjoy your retirement, don't you Mack?"

"Chief, they have her house under surveillance and bugged," Stone said, beating a dead horse to Chief's ears. "Who else knew Davis was coming home? They offed him because he wouldn't play ball with them Chief, I'm telling you. He served his bid and wanted to cut ties with the Feds. They had other plans..."

"Enough, Stone," Chief Taylor said, emphasizing the scope of Stone's allegations. "Just leave it alone. Go home. Get some sleep. Think about the beaches of sunny Southern California and leave it be. The Feds will handle this one. They'll do a great job to find their shooter, I'm sure of that."

FBI Offers Unannounced Award for Information of Informants Murder

The federal agency money will lure potential witnesses out of the dark

By Toriano L. Jackson of the Evening Whirl

The Federal Bureau of Investigation is offering a substantial reward for information for the arrest and conviction of the person or persons responsible for the murder of Darnell "The Dart" Davis. Davis, 29, was gunned down by a pistol-packing goon Tuesday night, just mere minutes after leaving his girlfriend's house in the Walnut Park neighborhood of North St. Louis.

Davis, a former standout basketball player at Northwest City High, had just returned home from a three-year prison bid earlier the day he met his maker and the Feds fear the killing may have been payback for Davis cooperation that brought down the infamous C.R.E.A.M. T.E.A.M.

Never ones to skirt the action of the streets, the FBI's office for the Eastern District of Missouri has announced an undetermined reward amount in an effort to bring witnesses forward.

"We're hoping somebody somewhere knows something and will voluntarily come forward," said FBI Special Agent Ryan "Guilt Free" Reynolds, a former detective with the St. Louis Police Department. "The reward will help."

Reynolds said, "The bureau's urgency stems from the fact Davis was a Federal informer, and while the 'hood don't tolerate snitches, the Feds love 'em."

"Darnell Davis was a key witness to a federal investigation and he had paid his debt to society. He was a young man trying to change his life and he didn't deserve to die with such ruthlessness."

None of us do, Agent Reynolds. None of us do.

THE PRIDE OF ST. LOUIS

When I first saw the 2005 schedule for the St. Louis Bulldogs, the semipro football team I've been a member of since 1999, I was stoked. After last season's horrifying playoff lost to the Springfield Rifles (the game was called with eight minutes to go in the 4th quarter with the Rifles ahead 40 something to 8; a bench clearing brawl prompted the cancellation) I swore I was done playing football.

After all, the prospects of receiving a professional tryout from the various pay for play leagues around the country were becoming dimmer as time passed.

The schedule, which I went online to peruse back in April, featured games against teams in Memphis, Chicago, Kansas City, Lincoln, Nebraska and the city that pique my interest the most, Dallas, Texas.

I'd had fond memories of Dallas. Back in the summer of 1994 I was part of a select college level baseball team that won the Missouri State Championship and advance to regional play in the Land of the Cowboys. While there, I had a chance to soak up the nightlife of Dallas, meet some ladies and do what most soon to be adults do--make irrational decisions.

After a few hours of boozing it up with my Denny's teammates, (the name of the select baseball team) on a dare from one of them, I got a tattoo. On the inside of my wrist sits a set of crap shooting dice, with a banner between them that reads: NATRUAL SEVEN, that's a lifetime reminder not to overindulge alcoholic beverages. Never in my wildest dreams did I ever thought I'd have a tattoo, but it fit right with the rebellious streak that pervaded that particular realm of my existence.

On top of those memories, an ex college roommate from Tulsa, Oklahoma, Marcus Carliss, had relocated to Dallas and I hadn't seen him in a few years. I had gotten his number from a mutual friend in Kansas City, touching basis with him every so often to talk about life situations and old memories living in Warrensburg, Missouri, home of the Central Missouri State Fighting Mules.

"Lil Nigga, what's up dirrty?" I spoke into the cell phone, referring to Marcus by the nickname bestowed upon him by a few CMSU football teammates. "What's cracking wit'cha'?"

"TeePee," Marcus responded with vigor, "what's up homie, what's going on?"

"Aw man, nothing," I prolonged, "jus' callin' to let you know I'ma be in yo' town June 11th."

"Oh word," Marcus said, "for what? You still ballin'?"

"Yes sir," I proudly replied, "still looking to get that ring, dirrty."

Marcus just laughed. He knew that the crew of brothers we linked up with as CMSU footballers always wanted some sort of championship ring to take with us to our football graves. We never got one at CMSU. Marcus, however, did.

After transferring from CMSU in the fall of 1995, he was part of a National Association of Intercollegiate Athletics national football championship at Northeastern Oklahoma State University in Tahlequah, Oklahoma. The luck of the draw is what we called it.

"T.P., man you crazy," he said. "How old are you now?"

"Thirrty one, dirrty, but I tell errybody I'm thirrty for life," I responded with a country grammar slur.

"There you go putting them extra r's in everything," Marcus chided, "sounding like an outtake from a Nelly video."

Marcus and I had a history of making fun of each other's dialect. He was born and raised in Los Angeles, moved to Tulsa as a teenager and relocated to his present digs in Dallas.

All of those cities tend to have a proper talking dialect whereas in St. Louis, no matter the intelligence level, most brothers speak with a verbiage now dubbed Country Grammar. Back in the early to mid-nineties, out of town brothers used to simply call our speech outback, down south and country.

"What I tell you 'bout how we live up herre dirrty?" I joined the verbal conflict. "Ain't nuthin' country 'bout my city, cuzz. We gangsta gutta up herre."

"Whatever," Marcus continued the jostling, "ya'll still ain't LA. You want to talk about gangsta? Now, LA is gangsta."

Marcus was a running back and I a defensive back in college. Playing those different positions sparked a natural rivalry between us, but it wasn't a jealously type thing. It was purely competitive. True to form, I egged the spat on.

"LA?" I countered, "LA? Man, Lil Nigga', you ain't lived in Cali in umpteen years, nigga. What'chu talkin' 'bout LA?"

"That's alright though," Marcus stood firm, "LA's in my heart. In my blood. I'm always LA."

"Nigga, you from Tulsa, Oklahoma," I teased.

"It's all good, though, T.P.," Marcus said in fun, "where ya'll playing at and at what time?"

"Man, I' on know yet," I explained, "but when I find out, I'ma call you and give you the heads up."

"Alright," Marcus said, "Cool. Just hit me up and let me know the deal."

"No doubt," I said.

"Alright, peace," he concluded.

"One luv," I wrapped up. "Holla at'chu ina minute

****

The trip to Texas to take on the Dallas Diesel in a semipro football game had all the makings of a bonding outing for the St. Louis Bulldogs. St. Louis' winningest minor league football team ever had struggled with their early preseason games in 2005, losing the first three to opponents deemed very mediocre by Bulldog standards.

The team was in the midst of a rebuilding process, having lost key members from the previous year's 8-4 club, including the star quarterback, running back, and wide receiver.

The dwindling out of players and coaches caused a ripple effect for St. Louis, leaving them in a rebuilding stage and struggling to stay competitive in a fledging semipro league.

Feeling a lack of cohesion on the part of the 2005 squad, Bulldog coach Greg Moore reserved a charter bus for the 12-hour ride to Dallas. The plan was to meet Friday, June 10 at 11:00 PM in the North Oaks Shopping Plaza, a local strip mall with retail stores and a bowling alley, and leave for the trip at midnight.

St. Louis would then arrive to its' destination by noon Saturday and have a few hours to eat a pre-game meal and maybe watch a movie at a local theater in Dallas. In typical St. Louis fashion, most of the team's players didn't arrive until well after midnight and Moore was peeved.

"Listen up guys," Moore ordered as players milled around the parking lot for a team meeting prior to boarding. The chief of Northwoods' (MO) police department, Moore was used to giving orders.

What ticked him off were guys not following the procedure he'd laid out for them.

"Some of you don't know what it means to be a St. Louis Bulldog," continued Moore, the Bulldogs' veteran coach of thirteen years and minor league football hall of fame member. Moore, all of five feet, six inches of him, was appalled. The three losses, even though preseason games, weighed heavily on him. He had scheduled the game against the Diesel thinking he'd have a squad that would compete for a national championship. Never did he imagine he'd have to go to Dallas with practically a rebuilt offense and minus several key defensive reserve players. He let the team know his feelings.

"We're going down here to play one of the better teams in our league," Moore scolded, "and we've only got thirty something guys here."

"Thirty one, Chief," tight end and captain Wendell Mosley informed.

"Thirty one," Moore corrected.

"Chief," Mosley chimed in again, "we ain't got to sit here and wait on none of these cats." Mosley, along with Moore, offensive tackle Stan Johnson and defensive end Fred Robinson, were the faces of the St. Louis Bulldogs.

They represented St. Louis at most of the NAFL's league functions, including all-star games and award banquets.

Moore gave them a certain leeway others players couldn't quite grasp. "Fuck 'em," Mosley continued. "Let's go. One monkey don't stop no show."

"Yeah, Wendell, you're right," Moore agreed, "but I hate to go down there with thirty one players. We want to make an impression. We need all fifty of our guys--there's power in numbers, boy."

"Guys," Moore said to his team, "get on the phone, call your buddies whose not here and tell 'em to get here. We need bodies. We need numbers, baby. Tell 'em if their having problems with the sixty dollar boarding fee, don't worry about it, we'll get it from later. Tell 'em to just come on."

At 1:40 AM, St. Louis headed for Dallas with just thirty-three players

****

What's up dirrty," I said into Marcus' cell phone the early evening of June 10. "You get my email?"

"Uhhh, um, I sure didn't T.P.," he unsurely replied. "I didn't check my email today at work, homie."

"Aw, it's cool," I pressed on, "I was jus letting you know we gon' be leaving the Lou around midnight tonight and get to Dallas 'round noon tomorrow."

"Yeah? You know where ya'll playing at yet?"

"Yeah. We, um, we um, gon' be playing at Capel High, Cappell High, something, at seven o'clock."

"Cappel?"

"Yeah, Cappel High, seven o'clock. I'ma call you when we touch down in the D, aw'ight?"

"Cool. Just call me and let me know when ya'll get here. I'll be around."

I was excited. I hadn't seen Marcus in quite some time and I wanted to catch up on old times and maybe get a chance to meet his two-year daughter who I hadn't met yet. He was astonished with my answer when he asked me the age of my son, Toriano II.

"How old is Lil' T, now?" he had asked.

"Twelve," I proudly stated, flashing a wide grin through the phone only a father could muster.

"Twelve!" Marcus deadpanned. "Damn, time is flying by. I know you got him playing ball?"

"Aw, man, football, basketball. I was going to let him play baseball dis' summer, but he been actin' a fool in school."

"What?"

"Yeah, dirrty, actin' a fool. Tellin' the teacher things like, 'so, you can't tell me what to do."

"You know what they say, right," Marcus cajoled.

"What?"

"The apple doesn't fall too far from the tree."

"Aw, nigga, gone wit' dat bullshi"t.

****

After a little over thirteen hours on the road, St. Louis arrived in the Dallas area around 2:30 on the afternoon of the 11th. The team had hotel rooms reserved at a Super 8 in Lewisburg, Texas but had stopped a few miles short of the destination to eat a light lunch before reporting to the high school stadium in Cappel.

The majority of coaches and players had slept through the night, including the two chartered bus drivers who took turns behind the wheel. Not Moore, though. He spent the trip trying to figure out a way to get his anemic offense to fire on all cylinders. Realizing the time was getting short,

Moore informed his players to fend for lunch for themselves, but report back to the chartered bus in one hour. Accordingly, players split up into familiar factions and dispersed into the humid and hazy Texas afternoon.

"One hour, or you won't suit up tonight," Moore barked to the fleeing crowd, "and I mean it damnmitt

****

I had slept through most of the nighttime part of the trip, even sleeping through a rest stop one of the two bus drivers we used made in the heart of Oklahoma. When I did finally open my eyes, I started recognizing parts of Oklahoma that I'd seen before.

As the procession moved forward, I spotted a green highway sign that read 'Welcome to Tahlequah'. I had visited Marcus there back in 1996 when he was playing ball at NSU and the sights of the town were forever engrained in my senses.

"Man, I knew dis' shit was startin' to look familiar," I said to my teammate, Arthur Meredith, sitting in the aisle seat right next to my window seat.

"What'chu mean?" Art pondered.

"My homie used to play ball down herre at um, Northeastern State back in the mid-nineties," I recalled. "Right herre in Tahlequah wherre we at."

"For real?" Art asked, pretending to be interested in my speech.

"Yep, back in '96-97," I explained. "Me and my homie Ping from Kansas City came down herre to check him out."

"Where you know that nigga from, dawg?" Art festered.

"Aw man, we went to Central Missouri together for a minute," I detailed. "Nigga transferred 'cause the coach wouldn't give him dat rock. He living in Dallas right na'. I'm finna call him and mess wit him, watch."

Instead of calling Marcus at ten in the morning, I decided to send a text message to tease him about his three-year stay at NSU. It read: 'We just past a sign that says Northeastern State University. What you know about Tahlequah?'

The reply: 'I'm a legend in Tahlequah, homeboy, what you know about it?'

My reply: 'I'm already knowing, dirrty, I'm already knowing.'

****

Once St. Louis reached their temporary living quarters in Lewisburg, they were forced to get ready for the game at the hotel because of the impending schedule change, courtesy of the Dallas Diesel.

"They want to start the game at six thirty because they got a film crew to video tape the game," Moore explained to his troops. "So, let's get our stuff on in the rooms and be ready to be on the bus at four thirty."

****

"Lil' Nigga, what's good homeboy?" I screamed into the hotel room's phone. "I'm in yo' area, cuzz."

"Word?" Marcus wondered, "Ya'll just now getting here?"

"Yeah, man, that's how the Bulldogs roll, baby," I tried to convince. "Check it. The game's been moved up to six thirty, so get therre on time so you can see yo' boy get his issue off."

"Alright, homie, I'll see you at six thirty then."

"Aw'ight, one.

****

The game was a disaster for the Bulldogs. Dallas came out smoking and after being held to a punt on their first offensive series, exploded for 18 points in the first quarter. By halftime, the score was 31-0 and Moore was fuming.

"You mean to tell me, these guys are thirty one points better than us?" Moore admonished the team. "I'on believe that. Just like they scored thirty-one, we can score thirty-one. Defense. That's it. You gotta hold' em to a shutout in the second half. Offense. Let's get our butts in gear and put some points on the board, damnmitt.

Moore's speech was short-lived. On the ensuing kickoff to open second half play, Dallas took the kick and ran it back 70 plus yards for a touchdown. The extra point made it 38-0 less than a minute into the third quarter. By all intents and purposes, St. Louis was done after the touchdown return. Much to Moore's chagrin, the final score was Dallas 73, St. Louis 0.

"We came down here and laid an egg," Moore bellowed from the throes of the post game meeting on the chartered bus. He gave instructions for the final phase of the trip. "For all you guys who came down here to party and enjoy the night life just know at eight o'clock tomorrow morning we're leaving. If you're not on this at bus at eight o'clock, you butt is going to be left here in Texas, damnmitt

****

"TeePee," Marcus called out me after our 73-0 whipping from the Diesel. "Looking kinda slow out there, homeboy,"

"Lil' Nigga!" I yelled back, playfully tugging at Marcus' midsection, "what's up my nigga? Look at'chu nigga, done got all fat and shit on me. You in love, nigga?"

"Man, gone," Marcus suggested. "What's up for the night? What ya'll got planned."

"Aw, nigga, dis' yo' town, we jus gon' get in where we fit in."

"Yeah, but what ya'll wanna do?"

"Man, I'on know, but hey look, pull ova therre to wherre dat bus is. We got a team meeting right now, and Coach is already mad

****

The trip didn't turn out as well for St. Louis as Moore wanted it, but he was still glad they made it. He preferred to travel with fifty plus players, and considered canceling the trip at the last minute. Not to show up at all wasn't feasible when St. Louis had thirty-three players capable of matching up with the Diesel. Unfortunately, the Diesel handed the Bulldogs the worst defeat in their history.

Exhausted from the trip, Moore slept through about twelve of the fourteen hours of the return trip, opening his eyes only for a quick peep at the game film and to grab a bite to eat.

Once the team's chartered bus reached North Oaks, Moore was livid again, and informed the team their practice routine of Wednesday and Thursday evenings had been adjusted.

"We want to see how many of you jokers show up on Tuesday," Moore challenged, "to work on your game

****

"Man, Lil' Nigga it was good seeing you again, dirrty," I said to Marcus as we arrived back to the Super 8 in the wee hours of Sunday morning. We had been out after the game at a local pub, having a few beers and chit chatting about old football stories. "You gon' hafta come up to St. Louis and kick it wit us sometime soon."

"Definitely," Marcus assured, "definitely."

"Aw'ight, my nigga, I'ma call you sometime while we on the road tomorrow to let you know all is good," I concluded, reaching out to Marcus to exchange the endearing handshake and hug widely practiced in the urban community. "'Preciate errythang."

"Ya'll be safe, T.P.," Marcus advised, "and get in that weight room. Those Texas boys were a little bigger and stronger than ya'll."

SECTION III:

GONZO BLOG ENTRIES

Definition of Gonzo

The Winds of Change

Butterflies

(I Wonder If I'll Ever See Her) Again

Catch Me Now (I'm Fallin')

Hanging By a Moment

Follow Me

(My) Definition of Gonzo

The gonzo form of writing is often characterized by the use of humor, exaggeration, profanity and drug-fueled rants aided by a stream of consciousness technique, and includes overlapping themes of sex, violence, drugs, sports and politics. It often blurs the line of fact and fiction, making for one wild and unpredictable ride weaving through a story.

THE WINDS OF CHANGE

The winds of change had swept through my boy Leon Moody so quickly, so briskly, that I had a hard time believing it was real.

I mean, it was only a few hours before when we had had the time of our young lives binge drinking, pot smoking and tactically plotting our enemies' demise.

Although we were five deep at the time of the accident, it was only Moody and I at Regional Hospital. Everyone else was spread out at other emergency rooms across the metro.

Moody set the wheels in motion.

"Thank you, God, thank you Jesus," Moody had painstakingly screamed from the throes of Regional's emergency room. "For I know you saved us God, father Lord, you saved us."

Consider for a minute Moody was a pot-smoking, beer guzzling, skirt-chasing, college football playing, gang-banging, weed-dealing, crack-slanging, hustling fool, the phrase 'Thank you, Jesus,' was as foreign to me as a South St. Louis youngster - like myself - taking up space in Russia, China or Japan.

Moody uttered the phrase shortly after the both of us had arrived at the hospital. Although I knew deep down the pain was real - everything about the homeboy was authentic - the phrase still threw me for a loop.

Trauma - especially the trauma Nose, Eric, Terry, Moody and I had just experienced - will knock you off your rocker for just a tad.

Laying up in that emergency room was a life-altering ordeal, so I could pardon Moody's sudden outburst. We were so close to death that God was probably the only thing that could have saved us.

Still? Gangster Moody, though?

I rejected Moody's conversion for the longest time. Who would I tote up with? Drink with? Cajole the females with? Hit the blocks with?

Shortly after that December, 1994 disaster, Moody went back to the community college in Illinois he was home from when we had our accident. I had left the City to play baseball at Jefferson County Community College in Hillsboro, Missouri. Moody and I talked often. One day, he called.

"I've changed my life, bro," Moody calmly said, as confidant as he was the first time I had met him during our recruiting trip to Central Missouri State University in Warrensburg some two years before. "I done gave up drinking, smoking and all that. I'm out. I'm out the game, bro."

In my own selfish way, I didn't want to hear that. I wanted my homeboy to be that same effervescent, outgoing ladies' man he had been since I'd known him. I still wanted him to bang those blue and gold gang colors, tote pistols and smoke the finest cheeba with me, his boy. I wasn't sure if I could handle a straight and narrow Leon Moody.

I put his newfound faith to task during that phone call. I knew he was in Palatine, Illinois playing ball for Rainey Harper Junior College, but he'd soon visit St. Louis again. He had too. That's where his family and friends resided.

"Aw'ight," I strongly countered, "that's all well and good, but them Six-Dukie niggas ain't gonna want to hear that shit, cuzz. What happens if one of them cats we been beefing with run up on you and you ain't bangin' no more. Huh, cuzz?"

"You know what, bro?" a cool as ice Moody said. "I'm going to leave that in God's hand that if them brothers see me they gonna have it in their hearts to know I ain't with that stupid stuff no more. I'ma leave in God's hand, you know?"

And with that, I knew the gangster Moody was no longer. I knew he was legit and I would never question his faith again.

BUTTERFLIES

For the life of me, I honestly cannot remember this young lady's name - Tabitha or Tamika or something or another - but she gave me the most exhilarating, yet unsettled nervous feeling I had ever known. At least since grade school, anyway.

I had met her in the early part of 2001. I know it was early 2001 because I was still working at Harold Pener's Man of Fashion store at Northwest Plaza in suburban St. Louis. The young lady had come into the store wearing the coolest Vokal lettermen's jacket on the market.

Initially, I was just going to do my job, greet her and her company and asked them, her specifically, if my help was needed. Instead, I went into full-fledged 'Mack-Daddy' mode.

"Hello," I suavely said, "welcome to Pener's Menswear. Let me know if you guys need any help today." Before I could finish my sentence, my thoughts went immediately to the next line of questioning.

"Damn, that's a nice letterman's jacket you got thurr, baby girl," I said to my temporary object of desire. "Whurr you find that?"

She was short by a woman's standard, petite and cute as a button. She had banana-colored, reddish skin, jet black her, a wonderful smile and seemed to be the sweetest thing on earth. I couldn't tell what her body looked like because of the lettermen's jacket and sweatpants, but my boy Nose would later observe she had a body 'like a 12-year-old boy.' To this day, I still don't know what he meant.

"Oh, my friend Yomi made it for me," the honey-baked scarlet said. "Why?" she blissfully continued, "you like it?"

"Hell yeah," I managed, "that mug is hot. I want me one."

"I'm prettty sure you could probably get one made," she replied. "Yomi takes custom orders. He'll make one for you."

"You got a number on dude?" I asked. "I want to put my order in. You think he'll make me one?"

"I'm sure he would," she reasoned. "Give me a pen and a piece of paper. I'll give you his number."

"He ain't gonna be tripping, is he," I countered, knowing full well St. Louis cats act a fool when random people call their line.

"No. Yomi's a business man," she assured. "He's mad cool. Just tell him I gave you his number and you guys can go from there."

After exchange a few more pleasantries, a couple trips around the store and some hob-knobbing, the cutie-pie asked me my name again.

"For real?", she affirmed. "No way. You and my boyfriend have the same name. No way."

Before she and her comrades left the store, I asked the inevitable, "what's poppin' tonight?"

She told me about a grand-opening party at Downtown St. Louis' newest hot spot on Washington Avenue. The party, she said, was going to be off the radar screen.

"I'm thurr," I said. Excited, I continued. I'ma look for 'ya, aw'ight? Don't tell me no when I ask for a dance either."

She flashed her pearly whites at me before heading out the store.

"I won't," she promised.

That night, I hooked up with my homeboy I played football and baseball with back in high school. Big Tone and I planned to hit the new spot together, but we both passed out around midnight on an over abundance of Belvedere Vodka mixed with crushed ice and cranberry juice and high quality herb we both had scored from our respective sources. By the time I came to, it was 2:30 in the morning. Quite naturally, the shindig was over. Damn, that was some good bud we smoked, I thought.

"Big Tone," I squealed as a gather my things from Big Tone's room at the family's home in East St. Louis. We had met on Park Avenue in South St. Louis after Big Tone had gotten off work at the sporting goods store his family owned, carpooled across the Popular

Street Bridge and stopped at Big Tone's crib so that he could get fresh and clean, boozing and drugging it up all the while. "Man, I had something hot waiting on me at the club. Damn. We missed the whole mutherfucking thang."

Over the next few weeks, I tried everything in my power to get homegirl on my team. I mean, I used to see her at all the hip-hop functions--the Spotlight Niteclub, Nelly shows, parties and concerts, celebrity-filled basketball games at Mathews-Dickey Boys and Girls Club and Washington University and more. We'd talk briefly on the phone, but never about any substantial. She always had an excuse for us not to hook up and chill. I didn't trip on it though. I wanted her and I wasn't going to be deterred by a little game of 'cat and mouse', you know? I mean, the few times we did run into each other after meeting, she was always cordial and polite, prompting those nervous little bubbles in the pit of my gut like some young school boy scarred to make a move on a girl he liked. It never failed. Don't know why, but the girl made me feel funny inside. A good funny, though.

Anyhow, to make a long story short, baby girl had this hold on me for at least three months and we never dated. Not once. No dinner, no movie, no trips to the Zoo, Science Center or nothing. Just chance meetings in public. I still dug the shit out of her, though.

One night I was - to borrow a phrase - out and about town. I had heard on the radio that a rapper with a hit song produced by Dr. Dre was going to be at the Spotlight. At that point, baby girl was the furthest thing from my mind, but was one of the first people I saw upon entry into the club. Her and a few friends were promoting a future show or what not when I saw her. Those same butterfly feelings took root. I hadn't seen her for awhile, but I was amazed those feelings of admiration were still inside me.

I was super cool in my approach. "What's up, baby girl," I said rather confidently, "you remember me?"

I just knew it was going to be all good between us that night. I just knew. Within seconds after saying hello, her transparent look through me was obvious.

"Oh my God, Oh my God," she screamed, fanning herself with her promotional flyers. "It's...it's...it's Knocturnal! Oh my God!"

Knocturnal? I thought. That fool has one hit on the radio and this girl is acting like she just seen Jay-Z or Puff Daddy or somebody. Knocturnal, though?

"That's what you get," Nose told me later. "I told you, dude, that broad wasn't for you."

(I WONDER IF I'LL EVER SEE HER) AGAIN

Kams is what I liked to call her. Family, friends and co-workers called her by her given name, but I preferred Kams. Her college soccer buddies had given her that name and I thought it was cool. My college football buddies had bestowed a moniker on me, so I could relate.

I had met her the first day on the job, but nothing that first day would indicate to me that this young lady would impact my life as much as she did. I can't say exactly how we hit it off, but it started out as a group of four young hungry journalists doing lunch together over all-you-can-eat Chinese food at the local China King.

Bob was the eldest of the four. Pushing thirty or maybe pass it, Bob was a cool customer. He had not a journalism degree, but a penchant for writing. He was a published author, and that, in a way, made him the de facto ringleader of the crew. Just short of six-feet tall, Bob had a low, curly flock, pale skin and an on again, off again 5 o'clock shadow.

Melissa. Wow. By my standards, Melissa had a great ass, was Polish and always...always cracked jokes about her Polish ancestry. Red hair, spects and freckles dominated Melissa's appearance. She was a tenacious, bubbly sort, convinced journalism in this tucked away suburb was only a start for her. She was intent on going back to her hometown of Chicago as soon as she could find a writing gig there.

Then there was Kams. She was of medium female height--exactly 5-foot, 5-inch fireball who usually got her story. She had long, free-flowing hair, was of Italian descent, studied Sciencetology or Christian Science or something like that and as I would find out later, adored me to no end. Those feelings were unbeknownst to me

150

for the longest time. Kams too had a great ass, a gorgeous body and enough spirit in her soul to lift me to heights I would have never known.

Those earlier lunches were great team building experiences as each of us was responsible for our own zoned editions. We were also responsible for writing six stories per week for the weekly community paper, covered city hall and school board meetings and had to make sure we had enough copy to fill the pages of our papers. We challenged each other to do better each week.

After a while, Kams and I would ditch Bob, who was happily married and Meliss--as Kams called her--would playfully ditch us in return. Kams and I started our own little lunch hour escape to some of the finest restaurants The County had to offer. Italian joints, bar-be-que shacks, mall anchoring Mexican cantinas, soul food eateries and yes, the reliable Chinese buffet. We progressed to dinner dates and social functions. On more than one occasion, we went to a Friday night hip-hop shindig at the Blueberry Hill in the Delmar Loop area of St. Louis County and partied like there was no tomorrow.

On Father's Day 2001--I had two sons, an 8-year-old and a 2-year-old--Kams took me on a weekend excursion to her parents' lake house in Cuba, Missouri, a trip I would never forget. Kam's family -- mother, father, younger brother, the mother's mom, both of the father's parents and the requisite "gay uncle" and his lover -- were all there. They were the nicest set of people I had met since my Eureka days back in the early 1990's.

Kams had warned me about her grandparents' reluctance to my visit. She explained that her father had reservations too, but she let me in on how her mother, who was just as cool and feisty as Kams, was all for the trip. Man, I had a ball that weekend taking in the amenities of a lake house in the middle of Missouri's Interstate 44 corridor. Jet skiing, white water rafting, we did all of that. I wasn't one to deal with nature's domain, but the experience enlightened both Kams' family and I.

On the ride back to the Delmar Loop area where Kams shared a two bedroom apartment with a friend, I kept telling Kams about how much fun I had. Smiling, damn near blushing, all she could muster was "I told you that you would enjoy yourself." She was right, though. I had enjoyed myself quite well.

Nearly two months after the trip to the lake house, I was unceremoniously dumped by the media outlet Kams and I worked. She was so outdone by the way I was treated that she tendered her two weeks notice the Monday after the Friday I was dismissed. "I don't want to work for a company that treats people that way," was Kams reasoning.

I didn't want Kams to quit. Times were getting hard and journalism gig opportunities were few and far in between. The writer's job market was tough and I knew that it would be difficult for Kams or me to secure quickly another job as a fact-finding, information gathering scribe. However, Kams was adamant about her resignation. Undeterred, she went through with it.

In some ways that was the end of Kams and I. The bond that ties was unilaterally pulled from underneath us. We went through the old song and dance about hooking up and hanging out, but slowly we drifted apart. We kept in touch for a short minute. After a few months of not corresponding with each other, I decided I wanted to see her so I made a call to Kams' cell phone number. I wanted to talk to her, invite her down to The City's Southside to show her how I was living since the dismissal. A few months before, when Kams inquired about my upbringing, I simply said "Naw, I don't think the 'hood ready for you."

That time was different. I wanted to see her, even if it meant her coming to visit me down by the old stomping grounds on Park Avenue.

"Hello," the pleasant voice on the other side of my phone line said.

"Kams," I replied. "How are you?"

After what seemed an eternity, I got an earful of hurtful scorn and extreme disgust.

"Why are you calling me now," the now sullen voice said. "I've moved on," it continued. "I share an apartment with my guy and I don't think it would be a good idea that you call me."

Kams' borderline sobbing went on.

"He knows about you. I've told him about us. It would not be right to see you. Please. Please don't call me again. There is just too much pain still there, okay?"

CATCH ME NOW (I'M FALLIN')

I don't know why everybody close to me - friends, family and associates - thought I was in love with Keva. She was just mad cool and fun as hell to hang out with. In my experiences, she was probably the most exciting relationship I'd ever had. Being with her was an intoxicating, drug-induced euphoric trip through the streets of the metro.

I had met the jolly little freak-a-zoid at the County lock-up's unisex holding cell. She was very stunning in her fitted, faded blue jeans and rust-colored sequenced top with matching three-and-a-half inch heels.

Along with a younger cousin, I was headed to one of the metro's hottest nightspots for a re-election shindig the local hip-hop star was hosting for the incumbent mayor. The cousin and I had made a quick, drunken dash to the northern part of the metro's suburb, strapped with light green cannibus, blunt cigars, tall cans of Budweiser and a fifth of Belvedere vodka and cranberry juice. For all intent and purposes, the detour was to make due on a promise the cousin had made to me a few weeks prior.

"Man, TP, I got somethin' hot for us to run," the cousin had said.

"Whenever," was my response. "I'm down."

The plan for the excursion to the 'burbs was to pick up the young lady the cousin had described as 'hot ass shit and ready to fuck both of us' and take her to the local telly for some pre-party hanky-panky. If the dame was as hot as the cousin said, I even suggested we take her to the election party with us and pawn her off for some cash to some of the local dope boys and ballers.

"TP, you got some Mags," the cousin asked as we pulled into the hottie's driveway. "I left mine at the crib."

"Yes siiirrrr! Look right there in the glove compartment."

The hottie turned out to be lukewarm. She talked a good game, looked nowhere near as hot as I was expecting and continuously objected to a stop at the local Motel 6.

"I'm saying, though," the cousin prescribed. "You already knew what the deal was, babee. We some playas. We ain't got time for this. C'mon TP, take her back to the crib."

"Cuzz, I ain't taking this broad nowhere. She's getting the fuck outta my car. Baby girl. If you ain't talking about smashing then you need to raise up. We ain't got no time to be out here in the County, bullshittin'. We got a party to go to, huh, cuzz?"

"Damn right, bitch," the cousin chimed, "so bounce."

"Hmmmmppphhh!," the hot-is-not scuffed. "Ya'll niggas got me bumped. I'm calling the police. You niggas gon' take me back home."

I was undeterred by the threat until I saw her dial those emergency numbers.

"Raise up!" I demanded, pulling to the side of the North County Interstate I had just entered. "You need to find your own way back to the crib."

"Hello? Police. I want to report...."

"Okay, damn," I relented, shocked she had actually called the authorities. "I'll take you back to the crib, hang the phone up."

"You gon' take to me back to where ya'll got me from?"

"Yeah, just hang the phone up. We don't have to get Johnny Law in this."

"Whatever. Police? We on two-seventy and..."

"Bitch, give me this muthafuckin' phone," the cousin said, snatching the phone literally out of the vengeful vixen's ear. "You ain't finna be callin' no muthafuckin' police over no shit like this. We gon' take you back to the crib and that is that. You trippin'. You already knew and my people were coming out here to run that and you gon' call the muthafuckin' Jakes. TP she called the muthfuckin' Jakes on us, cuzz."

"That's yo' piece, that's yo' problem. Just tell me where to go to get this broad up out my shit."

"Go left on this exit right herre," the broad hissed. "Then make a right at the second stop sign."

Before we could say 'the Jakes', two of the County's finest swopped up on us, red and white cherries blaring, outdated sirens blasting.

"What ya'll pull me over for?" I screamed after a few minutes of on-the-scene interrogation from the officers. "I ain't did nothing."

"Noise ordinance," one of the brown and biege-color uniformed officer said. "I heard your muffler from a mile away."

"You tripping," I offered. "I just got my muffler fixed and I got the receipt to prove it."

"Hey, shut your fat mouth," the other County Brown said, getting reports back from dispatch on my wanted and driver's status. "You got warrants out the asshole, dick wad, your ass is going in tonight."

"Man, I got some punk ass traffic tickets and ya'll gon' act like this?"

"Yep. And your boy here got somebody that wants him, too."

"That ain't my boy, that's my motherfucking cousin."

"TP," the cousin reasoned. "Chill, man."

"Man, fuck that. We ain't even did nothing, cuzz."

The call from the not so hot chick to 911 wasn't traceable. The officers that pulled us over, pulled us over for just that: a loud muffler. Seems the old double-barrel Holley carburetor and glass pack dual exhaust system was too much noise for the boys to handle.

"Look, baby girl," I said to the dame as the officers placed me and the cousin into cuffs. "Take my whip and park it in your driveway. I'll come get it when I get out."

I had no idea when I was getting out of the clink. I had some dollars save up for bail money, but didn't know if it would be enough to handle failure to appear on traffic ticket warrants in three different municipalities, including one on the other side of the state. Still, I entrusted the not so hot chick with my '81 Chevy. Better with her than at the impound, I thought. If she was still angry that I had threatened to put her out of my car, she wasn't letting on.

"Nell, knows my number," she said with assurance. "Just call me when ya'll get out."

The sly smile she gave had given me second thoughts on the makeshift safekeeping plan for the Chevy, but I proceeded anyway.

"Man, look," I barked as I headed for the patrolman's car, "park my shit."

Stunningly, she obliged. When I got out of the County lock-up some fifty hours later, she had indeed parked my car with nary a scratch on the custom candy apple red-coated paint job. Nor was there a CD missing from my collection of gangster rap, classic hip-hop, 80' and 90's rock, new age R&B and soul.

I had introduced myself to Keva shortly after booking and processing. Nearly eight hours went by as Keva and I yacked it up about all the conceivable things one could laugh about inside the County clink. What's crazy about the whole thing is we never exchanged numbers that night. Only names and jokes about how clean we all were in preparation for the high-powered throwdown for the mayor. It wasn't until a week-and-a-half later that, by chance, our paths would cross again.

As I usually did after getting off work, I had stopped by the cousin's digs on the Southside, close to the southbound Interstate. The cousin shared the place with his sister and her boyfriend. Without the blunt cigars and beer to celebrate another day on God's good earth, I made a mad dash to a convenience mart nearby before my anticipated stop.

After putting in a request for two tall cans of Budweiser and a five-pack box of Swisher Sweets, I noticed a young lady who looked vaguely familiar. I tried to recall a name or face, but blanked out until she said "where I know you from?"

"Man," I replied, "I'm trying to think where I know *you* from."

"'Ion know," she said as I paid with cash for my items. "But, I know you from somewhere, what's your name?"

"My name? What's your name?"

"Keva," she said, looking less glamorous than the night I'd met here, but still radiant and mad cool. She had on sweat pants, old sneakers and an oversized t-shirt with a ball cap to hide her un-kept hair. She still had a certain sex appeal about her, though. Maybe it was the east coast accent she purposely threw out every other word. I don't know, but whatever it was, we hit it off.

"Aw'ight," I said, "Aw'ight. I got it. When were in the County lock-up together."

"When?"

"What'chu mean when? How many times you been locked up, damn? About a week or a week-and-a- half ago. We both was headed to the Freeman Bosley party at The Spot."

"Oh, okay," she blushed. "I remember you. Whatta you doing over here?"

"What'chu mean? I told you I'ma Southside dude and I was going to catch you in these streets. What's good? What'chu got popping tonight?"

"Nothing. I'm staying at home with my two kids tonight," she said, placing in her order of Newport Kings and a tall can of Bud Light.

"Where your kids at now?"

"At home with their daddy."

"Ya'll live together?"

"Long story."

"Oh yeah? Long enough to tell over a blunt? You smoke bud?"

"Yeah, but I gotta get back home to my kids."

"We just gonna go right around the corner to my people's crib for a few minutes and smoke a blunt. You remember my cousin? The lil' short dude I was locked up with?"

"For real? I remember him."

"How'd you get up here? You riding?"

"Naw, I walked. We live in Soulard."

"You walked? Whatever you got to do to stay sexy, I guess. I got you. I'll take you home after we smoke this blunt. Nell gonna be fucked up when he see your ass."

"Can you just bring me back here?"

"Damn right, c'mon."

How crazy was this, I thought, as we both got into the Chevy. Not in a million years did I ever think I meet something as hot as Keva in jail. Running into her at the store, though? I knew we were destined to kick it something fierce.

"Give me a light," Keva partially demanded, scoping the nondescript inside of the Chevy.

"Here you go," I said as I offered the in-dash cigarette lighter.

"You smoke?" she casually asked, rumbling through the CD booklet that was perched on the passenger's side seat before her arrival.

"No squares. No Black and Milds. Nothing but the 'scomma'."

"The who? You making up words?"

"The scomma, ma. Hydro? Good ass weed."

"Boy, you crazy," she said through a giggle. "Where dat shit at?"

"My peoples got that shit on deck," I said arrogantly. "He just waiting on me with the blunts."

"Boy, you crazy."

Keva described in detail her situation at home with her kids' father, Jerome. They had a girl, 5 and a boy, 2 and shared a spacious two-bedroom town home in the Soulard neighborhood of The City. They were in and out of love, she said.

"Look ma," I reasoned, about to be blowed to the hilt from brew and marijuana-filled cigars. "It's good. I know my role in society. I'm just here to get you to have fun and blow trees with me and my peoples. This what we do. Daily. I mean I got a job and all, but you are more than welcome, anytime."

"Dude, you crazy," she said, again with a giggle.

Going against one of my basic principles of life--don't fool around with a guy's girlfriend, ex-girlfriend or baby's mother--I made my move on the five-foot, seven-inch something like a cutie. Her ass was a bit flat, but she had a nice set of perky tits that I remembered thinking in the clink how I would like to put my face in them. Man, she was brown-skinned and sexy and looked half-way decent in sweats. Only halfway, though.

"Look, me and my peoples are going out on the town Friday night and we want you to hang with us. Get all G'd up, smoke a lil' herb, drank some drank and get down how we get down. You down with that? I want to see you all dolled up again."

"That might work. I'ma see what's up and I'ma let you know. Write your number down, I'ma call you Friday and tell you what's up."

"Damn right, that's what I'm talking about. Cuzzo! What's good? Baby girl riding with us Friday night?"

"It's all good with me, ma, you can even get the front seat."

"Nell, the front seat? Damn, ma, you get the front seat. You gotta roll with us now, my peoples just gave up his front-seat-at-all-times privileges for you."

"I'ma see what I can make happen, for real. Take me back to the Citgo."

The day was balmy, if not a bit blistery. The evening? A crisp early March chill overtook the air. Keva was smiling as we headed to the Chevy, laughing at the cousin's flirtatious overtures. She looked stunned when she actually noticed the candy coated paint job.

"Damn, your car wet," she mused. "It's been raining?"

"Naw, baby," I replied with a bit of swag. "That's that candy paint dripping like that. My shit just looks wet."

"Damn," she laughed, "I thought your car was wet for real. It got gold flakes on it, too? Boy, I told you, you was crazy."

Keva had just laid on me the best compliment the Chevy's paint job had ever gotten. Right then, I knew again we were going to hang out and be friends for more than a minute.

"You ain't even heard the beats, yet."

"TP, you silly. Take me to the Citgo, I'on wanna hear no loud speakers banging all in my ear."

"Man, I like the way you say 'TP'," I teased. "Say it again."

"TP. Why?"

"It just rolls off your tongue. Say TP again."

"TP, you crazy," she repeated, just as I dropped her off at the Citgo. "I'ma call you and let you know about Friday for real."

Hanging By a Moment

"Bitch!" I screamed whole-heartily at Keva. "Yo baby daddy 'bout to die tonight, ho!"

Barely three months after we met, the relationship between me and Keva had become unpredictably crazy. Her man at home, Jerome, was not happy to be left all alone with their kids the majority of his free time. The youngins were disposed to the home of the couple's family and friends while Jerome was out looking for Keva, who was taking up her free time hanging with me.

Our time together was fun, intense and went by extremely quick. A day with her usually went like this: wake and bake, screw, go to work, take a lunch break, drive Keva to friends or family's home near my job, (she didn't work, she slept in my car while I clocked in for a few hours) go back to work, finish work, pick a so fresh and so clean Keva back up from the home of friends or family, bake some more, comp some Belve and juice, hit the town, party up, bake some more and then screw. The screwing, of course, was the best part.

One day, the party on wheels came to a screeching halt. The deranged --yet rightfully so-- jealous-hearted father of her kids had chased me and his broad some twenty semi-odd blocks through the streets of South St. Louis, literally trying to run us off the road.

From Broadway Street and Lafayette Avenue in Soulard all the way up Lafayette to the Gate District's intersection of Louisiana Street and Park Avenue, the cock-strong, bald-headed, dark skinned son of a bitch tried with all his might to make us wipe out. He had just spotted the early 1990's Ford Probe I had brought after soberly wrecking the '81 Chevy that Keva had praised so often during our excursions.

As mad as I was when I wreck the Chevy, I was also blessed to get out what we call in the hood a "hot box" or a "cat car." That motherfucker was a police magnet and I was never spared the moment law enforcement caught a glimpse of the candy paint. At one point in late 1999, early 2000, I got pulled over seven times in six months. The candy paint paired with a broken speedometer and a 350 engine was not a good combination to ride indiscreetly.

Jerome had spotted us during one of his fact-finding missions to locate his broad's whereabouts. It was obvious to him his broad was cheating. The fact I called the home the two shared with the kids probably didn't help, nor did the fact I picked her up from their digs in Soulard, while he was there no less. Still, he hadn't put a name or a face on the man responsible for taken his children's mother on a three month adventure through creepville. Keva's three-days-at-a-time no call, no shows only made the man more furious. He had it in his mind he was going to find out the deal and he did. Right there at Broadway and Lafayette.

"Oh my God," Keva screamed prior to the chase. She was visibly shaken. Just seconds before we were laughing and giggling like school children, listening and singing along to the St. Lunatics' "Let Me in Now". "It's him! It's him!"

She was too afraid to look back over her shoulder from the passenger side of the Probe, but she made it clear we had been made.

I was cool, but a tad confused. Dumping the ashes of the second blunt cigar we had smoked that early summer evening, I asked casually "him who, baby?"

"Jerome!"

My heart sank. Adrenaline shot up, then I looked. "It's cool, we good, see what he wants."

"Fuck that," Keva screamed, "he's crazy. Let's go!"

"Man, I got this," I said, underestimating the fury that burned inside Jerome. "See what the nigga want."

I busted a southbound U-turn on Broadway, headed west up Lafayette when Jerome's inferno became abundantly clear.

"Keva," Jerome not so kindly screamed from the driver's side of the new model Chevy he drove. "You betta' get yo' ass home to these kids befo' I kill you, bitch!"

I tried to remain cool.

"Hey look," I reasoned to Keva. "I'ma pull over up there and let you out so you can get back to your kids, ma."

Keva had been hanging out with me four at least four straight days, even though I held a full-time job. She didn't care and I didn't either. On the nights we partied up to the wee hours of the morning, she would ride with me to work, sleep in the Probe until my lunch break and I'd drop her off to freshen up at some obscure destination before heading back to the gig. I'd pick her up later and we'd do it again.

"Naw, man," Keva screamed. "Just drive. He's crazy. Drive!"

So I drove. I mashed on the pedal a bit to gauge if Jerome was really intent on getting his main squeeze back in the fold.

"Where my cell phone at?" I spoke into the air. "I got to get Nell on the phone."

The damndest thing happened. I had removed earlier that evening the little .25 semiautomatic I kept stashed in the Probe for security purposes. It was a Friday. I had gotten off work around 2 in the afternoon and made a trip, Keva in tow, to Streetside Records in the Delmar Loop. A local rap group had scored a nice lick with Atlantic Records for the music giant to distribute their debut album and they were scheduled for an in-store appearance to promote their hit single.

The in-store was at 4, so Keva and I milled around at a few of the shops in the Loop, before we descended on Streetside. I was scheduled to interview the group for the newspaper I worked, so the in-store made it an all around better story.

Anyway, Keva told me about a talent show her younger sister was participating later that evening at Riverview Gardens High and we made plans to make it. I just had to run to the City after the in-store and put the strap away. Bad enough we rolling with blunts, brew and vodka, I thought. Damn sure ain't 'bout to go to no Moline Acres with a pistol.

Just my luck we made it back from Moline Acres unscathed, but caught in a middle of a cat and mouse game of Speed Racer with Jerome and his cruel intentions. The man had the look of kill in his eyes, I wasn't strapped and I definitely didn't know what Jerome had on him. So I made a few calls to the people I trusted most and nobody was answering. It's Friday night in the City and ain't nobody answering their cellies, I thought. Ain't that a bitch?

"Damn," I mumbled to the air again, Jerome side-swiping the Probe at Lafayette and Tucker St. "Nell ain't answering. Carly ain't at the crib. Ain't nobody answering my mama's phone. This nigga's trying to straight make us wipe out."

"Hurry up," Keva screamed again. "He's crazy. Drive. Go faster. Drive TP, damn."

"Look," I said, agitated at the circumstance I was in. Jerome had continued chasing us after the side-swiping at Tucker and now we were both on a top-speed sprint towards Jefferson Ave. I blew stop signs at the Interstate entrance and Mississippi St. and a red light at Jefferson. I honked my horn incessantly to warn on-coming traffic to take heed. "We just gonna make it to the hood and everything's going to be good."

As both the Probe and Jerome's Chevy made it through the intersection, Jerome tried another maneuver in the attempt to cause the Probe to lose control. I was going at least 75 to 80 mph up Lafayette. He had to tap out at least at 90 mph because he cut us off three times before I made my most aggressive move of the ordeal.

I had already blew past stop signs at California, Nebraska and Compton, headed for Park Ave. It was the summer of 2001. Somebody from the hood was out and more than likely strapped up. I didn't want to take the flair up to my stomping grounds but my instincts told me to get to the homeland.

At Lafayette and Louisiana, I was supposed to make a right to get to the hood but I was going too fast to make it. Had I tried, I firmly believe I would have wiped out. Instead, I hit the brakes, Jerome barreling down on us, dashing out of the way of the Probe's sudden stop. Alas, I thought, my opportunity for breathing room. Once Jerome passed us, I hit the Probe into reverse, spun out to head north on Louisiana, stopping at the corner of Louisiana and Park Ave.

"Hey man," I yelled to my younger brother and his posse of comrades. The young turks were milling about on the porch of the four-family flat that housed our mother as one of the tenants. Jerome had corrected himself and was giving chase down Louisiana. "Get this nigga up off me."

On command, the younger brother and his partners came out the cut with small guns, big guns, machine guns, I mean an cache of weapons fit for urban warfare.

"This nigga right here," I yelled, jumping out of the Probe, pointing Jerome out. Jerome had seen the convoy form from the flat's porch and managed to avoid the wrath. He drove past us, lowered his window down and screamed, "Aw bitch, you gon' get some niggas to shoot me."

"Give me the strap," I said to the younger brother. He held a Tech-9 semiautomatic that I knew would tear Jerome a new asshole. Before I could even consider squeezing the trigger, Jerome had vanished down Park Ave and was already at Compton Blvd. I turned my attention back to Keva. "Bitch, yo' baby daddy 'bout to die tonight, ho!"

FOLLOW ME

I had made the trip to Keva and Jerome's pad in Soulard many times. This time was different. Before, I was simply psyched to pick up Keva and hit the town on what would become countless missions of boozing, smoking and sexing. Now, I held a fury burning inside me that I had never felt before. It was a feeling of wanted to blow that cocksucker's Jerome head into smithereens with the six-shot .38 special I had gotten from my younger brother.

Moments before, Jerome had chased me with his woman in tow from Soulard all the way up to Park Ave. He tried in vain to make us crash. He had to pay for that, I thought. I'm going to kill that fool.

I traded with the younger brother the Tech-9 semi-automatic for the .38. I wasn't real comfortable toting a weapon like that around with me in South St. Louis. I needed something easy and compact, but nevertheless, I was intent on Jerome going down.

The funny thing about the situation is that I was as wrong as two left feet. I disrespected the man by going and calling his house. Although I took exception to the chase, in my heart, I knew I was wrong. I still made the trip to see that fool. I made Keva post up in my mother's house on Park Avenue, so there wouldn't be a witness to the massacre.

I literally retraced the steps to Jerome and Keva's house Jerome had chased us from minutes earlier. Speeding from Park to Compton to Lafayette to Soulard, I had time to formulate a game plan. I was going to simply bash that fool's windows out of his car until he came outside. Once he came to check the damage, I was going to let loose the six hollow point shells the younger brother had in the snub nose .38.

Parking the Probe deftly two blocks from Jerome and Keva's, I tip-toed through alley that lead to the back entrance of their town-house. I soon as I hit the corner, Jerome was in plain view, talking vehemently to a police officer parked in the alley in a paddy wagon. More inspection showed a regular police cruiser and another one tagged with the Mobile Reserve decal on it. One thing I know about the St. Louis Police is you don't fuck with Mobile Reserve. Those are some rugged ass cops.

I quickly did a reverse limbo out of sight. I had forgotten Keva told me Jerome acted so crazy because he had partners who were on the city's police force. Mobile Reserve to be exact. I got in my Probe and headed back to Park Ave. I was still furious and I still had plans on fucking up Jerome's melon with hollow points.

"Big Bro," the younger brother said as I scurried back to the Block. "What the fuck is up? You get that nigga?"

"Man, that fool called the motherfucking Jakes," I retorted. "Scary motherfucker. Where that nigga baby mama at?"

"She in the crib, sitting at the kitchen table. I had to give that bitch a bopper to calm down. The bitch was crying all hysterical and shit, talking about 'TP gon' kill my baby daddy, TP gon' kill my baby daddy.'"

"You gave that bitch a X pill, lil' brother?"

"Yeah, man, she was up in mama crib spazzing out."

"Aw'ight, lil' bro, it's cool. Go get that bitch. I'ma hold on to this .38 for the next couple of days, aw'ight?"

"That's cool. You do some dirty work, don't bring that mug back here. The block already hot."

After briefly explaining to the younger brother the reason behind all the commotion, I summoned Keva to the Probe, instructed her to roll a blunt and promptly berated her for having me in such a compromising situation. I blamed her that night, forgetting all about the role I played in the situation.

"I'm taking your ass, home tonight," I bellowed, knowing full well I wasn't ready to send Keva packing. "I'm done with this shit."

"No, TP, no," Keva protested amid tears and constructing another marijuana filled cigar. "I'on wanna go home. Jerome gon' kill me."

"I'm saying, what you want me to do," I barked. "That fool just tried to run us off the road because of you. I get rid of you, I get that fool off my back."

"Just let me stay with you tonight, TP," she suggested. "He's crazy and I'on know what he gon' do if you take me home. I'll just go to my momma's house in the County in the morning."

After thinking it over a bit, I realized the best sex in the world is mad sex. Or make-up sex. Or ecstasy-fueled sex. The way me and Keva got down, I thought, 'what the hell?'

"Aw'ight, we'll get a room tonight, but in the morning, I'm taking you so far away from me your head's gonna spin."

Needless to say, the sex between me and Keva that night was phenomenal. It was always good, but that night, I had a couple of extra aggressive pumps that made us both bust like the Niagara Falls. After laying up in the hotel room until checkout time, I made a quick dash back to Park Avenue to pick up some mail I was expecting at my grandmother's house. It was close to noon, the sun was out and so were the dope boys getting their mid-day hustle on. My mother and grandmother both were sitting on my grandmother's front porch when I pulled onto the block and parked the Probe across the street from my grandma's dwelling.

"Stay here," I demanded to Keva. "I'll be right back. I got to go check on to see if this mail I've been waiting on done came."

"Hurry," Keva said, looking a bit rugged from the all night bang session we had and still feeling the effects from the ecstasy pill the younger brother had given her to calm her nerves.

"Hey, Mama, Granny," I said, planting a wet one a piece on the cheeks of my favorite girls. "What's going on?"

"Hey baby," my mother said.

"What's going on with you," my grandmother said, giving me that look like she had heard about the activities the night before. "Whose that in your car with you."

My grandmother did not like Keva at all. They hadn't met, but I had sneaked Keva into my aunt's house countless times to rock her world and my aunt, a mother of twin girls and a pre-teenage boy, didn't approve. She basically ratted me out to my grandma.

"My friend," I said.

"Don't be bringing that little jezebel to my house," my grandma deadpanned. "I don't care for her at all."

"Aw Mama, leave that boy along," my mother said, protecting her second oldest like she always had. "You don't even know the lil' girl."

"Look, ya'll, I just came over here to get my mail. The mail man ran yet?"

"Yeah, he ran," my grandmother said, "and I told him you don't live her so quit delivering mail in your name to my house."

I got a kick out of my grandmother's ribbing, but I was in a hurry. I had no time for small talk. Hell, I even had the .38 tucked away in my waistband.

"Damn, baby I told you I'd be right back, what are you doing," I said to Keva. I had just retrieved my mail, used the toilet and was on my way back to the car when she appeared on my grandmother's porch. She had that look she had gotten we see saw Jerome the night before.

"I just saw him," Keva screamed out, pushing her way past my mother and grandmother. I don't even believe she spoke to them.

"Saw him where?"

"He just rode down the street and I think he making a u-turn."

"Tory," my grandmother called out. "What the hell is going on? Why is she running all up into my house."

"Ain't nothing, Granny, I got this."

"Well, whatever it is, ya'll need to get away from here with it. You know I don't play that mess."

I was in a jam. Jerome was outside lurking, I had a pistol in my pocket and my grandmother was not a happy camper. To make matters worse, my father, who lived around the corner from Park Ave on Eads Street had just made his way around the corner to cajole with my mother about their former lives together. How is this going to pan out, I thought.

"Granny, ain't nothing going on," I reasoned. "We about to go."

"I know ya'll about to go," my grandmother said. "Away from here please."

Before I could take one step off my grandmother's porch, the shit hit the fan.

"Bitch, you need to come home," Jerome screamed from the driver's side of the Chevy he had chased us down with. "I ain't playing with you, you got kids."

Keva did have kids. Two of them. And guess what? Jerome had them in the back seat of the car as he dressed down their mother perched in front of my grandmother's crib. I walked Keva past Jerome's car, across the street and let her back into my car. I approached Jerome. He was sitting in his car, driver's side to the street. I was in the middle of the street. I was livid. I was mad. Damn that fool didn't just try to run us off the road the night before, but now he was on The Block, disrespecting the whole situation. Cats in St. Louis should already know, you don't go to another cat's 'hood and start woofing. I reached into my waistband for the .38.

"Dawg, you need to get off this block," I said menacingly. I never brandished the pistol, but I had my hands on it. "You think this is a motherfucking joke. You need to bounce."

Jerome seemed oblivious to my demands. He wanted his broad to come home and he looked right past me.

"Bitch, you think this is a game," he screamed through me at Keva. "You need to get you' ass in this car."

At that moment I was too outdone. Taking aback if you will. The nerve of this fool to look past me like I wasn't standing on anything. I didn't have much, but I had an ego and some self pride that wasn't about to let that shit ride. Especially after the car chase.

"Nigga," I said again. "If you don't get of my block with all that bullshit, I'ma blow your motherfucking head off." Just as I was about to pull the pistol, I caught a glimpse of the young tikes in the back seat. My conscious would not let me pull the gun. My mother's out here, I thought, my grandma, my daddy. This nigga got the kids with him. Damn. "Raise up, nigga."

"Hold on, hold on," my mother screamed. She ran up to the passenger side of Jerome's car. "What is going on?"

"Hey, look Mama, I got this," I said. "This nigga needs to bounce."

"Look, Renee," my father said. "Let that man handle his business. He grown."

Now, I don't believe my father knew I had a pistol. I think he was just trying to convey to my mother that I could handle the situation without her bumping her two cents in it. He was right. I needed her and my grandma to chill out.

"Hey baby," my mother continued talking to Jerome. "If you need her to come home we gon' make sure she gets home, na. We don't want no problems."

"She don't wanna go home with that nigga," I protested as my mother and grandmother marched me out of the middle of Park Ave towards the Probe. My father sat back quietly and watched. "She scared. That nigga is going to kill her."

"Oh no, un un, you got to get up out of here," my grandmother said to Keva, literally trying to pull Keva out of the Probe. "Get out of my grandson's car."

"Hold on, Ms. Porter, don't be grabbing all on me," Keva said in protest. She was getting a bit too testy with my grandma for my liking.

"Hey, Keva, don't be talking to my grandma let that," I said. "Granny, let her go. If she don't want to go, she don't have to go."

During that exchange, my mother had convinced Jerome to make his way, but he gave me the most evil of all looks when he pulled off. I had never felt so angry in my life.

"C'mon," I said to Keva. "I'm taking you home."

Keva was dead set on not going home. She convinced me to take her where I said I would take her: to her mother's home in North County. We barley said two words to each other the whole trip.

"I'm going to holla at you later," I said as I dropped her off at her mother's digs. "Be good."

The ride back to The City was a tough one for me. I still had the .38 in my pocket. I still wanted to take Jerome's head off, but the look in his and Keva's children's eyes was enough for me to forget that thought. I just wanted to go somewhere, get out of the street and lay my ass down. I slept for the better part of the day. The next day, a Sunday, it all came to a head.

"Yeah, Mr. North County Journal," the voice said through my cell phone. It was early, I was emotionally and physically drained and I hadn't had my wake and bake yet. I was a bit agitated by the call. "I know where you work at, where you live at, where play at, next time I see you I'm putting that 9 milli to yo' head."

I knew it was Jerome. My first thoughts were, 'I'm going to have to kill this nigga.' In the same breath, I made a conscious decision.

"You know what, dirty, you sho' right," I said, relenting on the male piss test with Jerome. "I don't need to be messing with your girl. From here on out, playa, you don't even have to worry about me. I'm done. You can have those problems all to yourself."

I hated to say it, but I had to. It was coming to the point where I thought I was going to have to kill Jerome, prepare that he was going to kill me or wonder if he was going to kill me, then Keva, them himself. Either way, I'm no killer and I didn't want that blood on my hands. I damn sure didn't want to die. I waited on Keva to call me to break the news.

"Look, ma, you need to go home to your man and your kids," I said. "This here between us is over. It's done. Don't call me no more, we're through."

Keva went down swinging.

"No, TP, no," she said, "don't do this. Why you doing this?"

"Because baby, you need to get home to them kids. We had a nice little run. Now it's over. Be good."

Keva called my phone for the next two hours but I refuse to answer it. I was done and I meant it. Hell, Jerome called me for the next two weeks, still questioning me about his children's mother's whereabouts and levying threats.

"Look, man," I said to the crazed fool before hanging up. "I told you I was out of the picture. I ain't seen or talked to your girl. She probably done moved on to the next new nigga, dawg. She ain't with me."

SECTION IV:

POEMS

No Luv

Reflections

A Boy Named by Paul by Rory L. Watkins

Dearest Jesus by Rory L. Watkins

No Luv

I wanted to be a star, man, a star.
Not just any old star, but a football star.
You know, the kind of star that's on television every Sunday
Playing a kid's game for a King's ransom.
No Luv.

They wanted to be hood stars, man, hood stars.
Not just any old hood star, but real street stars.
You know the kind, pants sagging, mouth full of gold, tricked
out cars.
Dope dealing, gun-toting hood stars, man, niggas on the block
shining.
No Luv.

I loved putting on that Cardinal Red and Black uniform.
Not just any uniform, but the Cardinal red and Black uniform
of the Mules.
You know the uniform, shiny black pants, fit to a tee and the
Cardinal Red #5 jersey.
Damn, man, I used to look so sweet in that damn Mules jersey.
No Luv.

But things change so quickly, man, so damn quickly.
I still wanted to be a star, man, a star of all stars.
You know the kind, the star that shines so brighlty over all the
others.
Yep, a motherfucking star.
No Luv.

Them niggas wanted me dead though, man, dead.
Fuck that college shit, that football star shit.
Them niggas wanted me dead, man, dead.
Damn, man, them niggas used to be my homies.
No Luv

I'll show them niggas, man, they can't put my candle out.
I'm a star, man, and I'll continue to shine.
I got teammates, man, teammates, roommates, coaches and fans.
They know I'm a star, man and they'll keep my candle lit.
No Luv.

Them niggas couldn't get me the first time, man.
I'm still shining.
They got me the second time, man, now I'm dying.
Yep, I'm dying, but I'm still a star, man, shining brightly.
No Luv.

I'm good now, though, man, I'm good now.
I'm up here with all the other stars, man, destined to shine forever.
I look down and my guys on the Mules are shining, man, still shining.
I'm shining too, man, I'm shining too.
No Luv.

Dedicated to our fallen soldier, Wesley Maurice 'Milk' Drummond. We love you homie and we miss you like crazy.

Toriano L. Porter, circa 1998

REFLECTIONS

I really don't know where to begin this tale of evil distortion, you know, the kind the media blow out of proportion?

It probably began in "88 when some fool wasted Delancy, for goodness sake.

My older brother's main cat, the kinda nigga that whipped both our asses, three years back.

Got my big bro started in the game, and in return, taught me the same.

But, that's it. Smoked by a fool with grudge, and for shit.

Man, oh man, Wesley was next we called him Milk, because of his flex.

This cat was cut like a rock, didn't drink or do drugs, a straight up jock.

Walked on the football team as a freshman in college. By the time his sophomore year, he earned a full athletic scholarship.

Balled for two years; even started a few games, then came the tears, then came the pain.

On the streets of St. Louis celebrating the 4th of July. Why did somebody tell me my homie Milk had died?

In a all out frenzy, panic, if you will. I called around town to see if my homie had gotten killed.

They said it was false, but he did get popped, by some cold-hearted motherfuckers from his same damn block.

Shot two times in his iron-clawed hands, the homie Milk was told, he could never ball again.

Dejected and depressed he came back to school. But Milky had changed, he was acting a Got Damn fool.

Drinking and smoking weed, Milk did it all. Said he didn't give a fuck about nothing except for playing ball.
Went back to St. Louis to see a specialist. The cat wanted to play ball and he was getting restless.

Just so happened, I was at the crib too, skipping a couple of days, getting a reprieve from school.

But Low and Behold, what did I see on the news? A couple of cats wanted for making a 20-year-old college student sing the blues.

I couldn't believe it, I told Big Moms. She gave me that old speech talking about 'calm down, son!'

Fuck that shit, people thought it was me. But it hurt so badly to picture Milky dead in the streets.

Then came Meko, a wild-style from the block, the kinda cat with an attitude and a big ass glock.

Seem them boys in blue rushed in the door. Knocked Meko face down on the floor. Pursued with the raid, ripping shit up, then they claimed Meko got up?

Reached for a gun, in a room full of cops? Come on, my homie didn't really want to get shot.

They did a fine job of covering it up, but The Block went crazy, ready to erupt.

More boys in blue came out and so did blacks. On the prowl, on the attack.

What the fuck? Here comes the evening news, ready to report another homie singing the blues.

Oh shit, what do we have? A dead black man and neighbors on the warpath.

Lead story, front-page news, nobody called me to break the news.

Opened up the paper a few days late, have I lost another true soldier to this damn heartbreak?

To tell you the truth, I don't much know the facts, all I know is, 'Lil Damon turned up whacked.

Shot two times to the back of the dome, I had just seen the 'lil nigga when I last went home.

I said 'come back with me, cuzz, it'll be all cool, you never know, you might want to enroll in school.'

He said he'd bounce, but he would check me later, I said, 'it's all up to you, no less nor greater.'

I went back to school, 'Lil Damon missed out. I had to go, and he was nowhere to be found.

Struggling in school, two weeks had past, I called may Aunt, looking for his young hot headed ass.

"Oh, you ain't heard?' That's what my aunt said. 'About a week ago, they found him on The Lot dead.'

What a terrible way to learn of such a tragic death. Is it my entire fault? Maybe I shouldn't have left.

I really don't know the circumstances nor what really went on. I didn't bother to ask, I just thought, leave well enough alone.

I hurt to this day, I shed tears of pain. Oh, young cuzz, 'Lil Damon, just to see you again.

My next homeboy, was like déjà vu, he was capable of the same damn things that Milk could do.

Talk about your all-around star, Antonio Wadlington, 'BirdMan', used to do it all.

Sports, comedy or playing Valentino. That fool had a knack for putting on a show.

Wasn't a showboat, just straight-up real. Kept things loose but with a mass appeal.

Kicked it too much, got expelled from school. Back on those St. Louis streets, acting a Got Damn fool.

His gal came home, she found him dead, body all sliced up, face full of lead.

Bond and tied, I ask for what? Some dope fiends had robbed him, for what they tell me--sixteen hundred bucks.

If you see a pattern, surely you can tell why. In those St. Louis streets, it's straight do or die.

Dedicated to my fallen soldiers. You all are truly my angels. -- Toriano Porter, circa 1998

A Boy Named Paul by Rory L. Watkins

There was a boy named Paul and he was in the fourth grade. Paul lived with his mother and four siblings; his older brother, Jesus and younger siblings Veronica and Cochise. When Paul and his brother Jesus went to school they always stood out. Paul would wear the same clothes as the other kids were all wearing, but the other kids still made fun of Paul because his clothes weren't new; they were hand-me-downs from Jesus. Jesus clothes were from thrift stores.

Every time Paul left home he felt like he was just like the rest of the kids at his school because most of the kids in Paul's neighborhood told him he was one of the neater kids around there way. One day at school, Paul was told he had to go to a different meal line during lunch hour. Of course he didn't understand but he did what he was told and left it at that. Shortly thereafter, Paul became upset because he felt like he was being separated from the other kids because he used meal tickets for lunch and the other kids used money.

Curious to know, Paul asked his teacher, "why can't I use money for lunch like the other kids do?" One the other kids shouted out, "because you ain't got no money. Ya'll po'." That evening Paul asked his mother, "Mama, you got some money? I want to buy my lunch tomorrow." She replied, "Paul I'm broke as an old car window. Us poor people spend our money on bills." "Mama," Paul said, "them people on T.V. po', we ain't po'. We got a car and plenty of food in the fridge. We ain't po."

DEAREST JESUS BY RORY L. WATKINS

Dearest Jesus:

How is everything going? I truly hope this letter finds you in the best of health. My intention with this scribe is to enlighten you on the subject we were discussing on the telephone a couple of days ago. Son, I know times are really hard without having your father around, but my main focus is to help you understand my position. See, I wasn't born with a lot, but I can honestly tell you that I have never been poor. When I say poor or even when I think to say the word poor, I get scared son. Immediately. I become scared simply because I know that I never had a chance to instill in you the things my mother instilled in me.

You grandmother taught me so much, so many things that I never got a chance to share with you. When I was younger I thought that lacking the material items so prevalent in our society meant we were poor. Although my mother provided me with all the basic essentials of life like hot water, food, gas, heat and lights, I still felt beneath others because I wasn't wearing the popular name brand clothes and things of that nature. My mother sat me day one day in my formative years (12, 13 years old) and explained what being poor really meant. The dictionary defined poor as 'wanting in amount or less than capacity, or less than adequate.'

In ways, many of us are poor in our views of life. I am not speaking of money, but of state of mind. You all's generation of people are too 'poor' to ever be considered rich. Money is not a factor when you are limited in mind and soul and lack reasoning. When you do not

183

have the mental capacity to reason, then you lack educational arousal to exercise verbal skills. Continuing to believe that you are rich due to the readings on your bank statement will only feaster the suffering of a life long journey of being poor.

As humans we make mistakes and do not always see the big picture before judging others. The so-called lower class people may not be so lower class after all. They simply see life for what it is and have the knowledge to direct themselves in a direction that leads to emotional and spiritual prosperity.

Son, I'm sorry about the predicament I have put our family in, but I too was busy reading my bank statements and forgot what was really important: you, your mother and your brothers and my darling Veronica. I once had the same thoughts as you, but I never got a chance to turn things around. You, son, have the chance and I pray that you will take these words very seriously and do something to help your mother's situation.

Truly yours,
Your Father

SECTION V:

PREVIEW OF CIRCA 1985,

A Novel by Toriano l. Porter

CHAPTER 1: Adios Park Avenue

CHAPTER 2: Love at First Sight

CHAPTER 3: Hot Summer Nights

CHAPTER 4: A Brand New Day

CHAPTER 5: New Found Friend

CHAPTER 6: Field of Dreams

CHAPTER 7: JVL Posse

CHAPTER 1:
ADIOS PARK AVENUE

I had never heard of James 'Cool Papa' Bell nor the street that bore his name until my mother informed my brother Sonny and I that we were moving onto the North St. Louis street named after the Negro Baseball League great. Honestly, back then, my brother and I thought it was the silliest name a street could ever be named.

"What kinda name is that for a street any damn way," Sonny asked. Thirteen at the time, Sonny was very defiant towards our mother and he made it a point to let her know he didn't want to move from the City's Southside into the Jeff VanderLou housing projects.

"Boy, watch yo' mouth," Moms shot back, raising her hand with an open palm to warn Sonny he was on the verge of another classic beat down, "before I wash it out with soap and hot water."

"I'm just saying, Moms," Sonny countered, "I'on wanna move to no Northside. Especially no JVL. Them cats be illin'. Let me stay with Grandma.

I was a bit of a momma's boy, a titty licker, if you will. Wherever Moms was going, I was going, so I was cool with the move. Besides, everybody on Park Avenue already knew our dad, Pops Winston, played minor league baseball within the St. Louis Cardinals' organization, so a move North could only spread the news.

"My momma ain't trying to raise yo' hardheaded butt, boy," Moms said to Sonny. "She done raised her kids. So grab some boxes, go upstairs and start sorting yo' things. We otta here in three days."

Three days wasn't a lot of time for Sonny to do all the neccessary things he had to do; besides packing, he had about three different girlfriends he had to break the news to. One, Pam, was fifteen, so she was cool about it. Another, Monique was happy we were moving and the other, Niko, was heartbroken.

"Why, Sonny," Niko wondered, "why ya'll moving so soon?"

"Moms wanna be in the new spot by the first so we'll have a month before school starts," Sonny explained. "That way, we'll be all settled in by the time Pops get back to town."

Pops was expected to be a September call up by the baseball Cardinals. At 30 years of age, he figured he had put up decent enough numbers at Triple A Louisville to be at least an expanded roster addition and by all accounts, the Cardinals planned on just that.

"Does that mean I'll never see you again, Sonny?" Niko continued. "Does that mean we gon' break up?"

"Baby, calm down," Sonny consoled, "you know my Grandmother still lives on Park Ave, so I'll be seeing you again. So, let me get off this phone so I can start packing my suff."

"Sonny, wait, don't go," Niko pleaded. "I wanna tell you something."

"Niko, I gotta go, Moms 'bout to come in here tripping," Sonny said. "I'll call you later."

Moms was a tall, regal woman, albeit a little on the skinny side. She lived fast, played hard and didn't take kindly to disrespectfulness toward her, her kids or family and friends. Her and Pops had gotten married when she became pregnant with Sonny. Moms was just eighteen at the time, Pops seventeen and on his way being drafted by the Cardinals in the 20th round of the 1972 amateur draft. Despondent over his draft selection and subsequent signing bonus offer, Pops elected to go to the Community College in the hopes of improving his draft prospects. Two years later, the Cardinals drafted him again, this time in the 12th round and he signed.

The young couple struggled financially and by the time I was born in '74, Moms had moved back in with Grandma on Park Ave, while Pops toiled in minor league cities in Texas, Arkansas and Kentucky. We lived with Grandma off and on up until that August day in 1985 when we moved to the JVL.

That last day on Park Ave was an interesting one. Some of the neighborhood crew decided to have an impromptu baseball game between the Park Avenue Pirates and the McGinnis family in Terry Park, a neighborhood gathering place for kids and adults alike.

The McGinnis' were a family in the neighborhood that outnumbered everybody else's family three to one. They could fill out a baseball team by themselves and not just a nine man team. More like a 25 man roster. The Pirates were made up of everybody else in the neighborhood who weren't related to the McGinnis'. Although we had black Pittsburg Pirates with the P on the bill and matching yellow t-shirts, The Pirates struggled to fill a team of nine consistently. Sometimes we played with seven or eight people. Once, when we had only five people show up, the McGinnis' loaned us four of their relatives. That game ended up in a fight between us and our temporary teammates.

After taking ground balls and warming up, both teams were ready to go. We had umpires, bases, aluminum bats and a real league ball, courtesy of Pops. I made sure everyone knew it was my ball, by labeling it : "This Ball Belongs To Cassius Clay Winston." Marcus McGinnis didn't take too kindly to that.

As I stepped into the box to lead off the weekend annual contest, Marcus snapped.

"Why this lil' nigga got his name all over the damn ball for, man?" Marcus asked to no one in particular. "We know it's his ball. C'mon scrub, dig in."

Marcus McGinnis wasn't but a year or two older than me, but he was intimidating. He had a certain roughness to him that scarred the bejesus out of me and stepping into the batter box that afternoon was freighting.

"Strrrrike one," the home-plate umpire, Junior McGinnis, bellowed out as I watched Marcus' first pitch fastball buzz by. Junior was one of the older McGinnis' and he usually called the games from behind home plate. He had played ball with Pops at the Community College, so he thought he was the most qualified to call ball and strikes.

"C'mon, Cass, swing the bat, baby," my teammate and cousin Corleone said. "Swing the bat."

"Watch the fastball, Cass," my other cousin Lucky said, "he ain't got no curve."

"Ball!", Junior screamed out as Marcus' attempt to shut Lucky up bounced about three feet in front of the plate.

"I told you," Lucky teased, "he ain't got no curve."

I could tell that Marcus was getting mad for being teased about his curveball, but I knew he wasn't going to stop trying to throw it either, so I decided to take one more pitch before I swung the bat. Pops had always told me to be thinking two pitches ahead to counteract what a pitcher was trying to do. Marcus was trying to establish his curveball.

"Ball two!" Junior screamed as he dipped out of the way of Marcus' wild curveball. By then, his cousin and catcher, Mitch, was frustrated.

"Hey, man I ain't finna be trying to catch all these wild 'lil curve balls," Mitch informed, "so throw some heat."

By the time Marcus flung that 2 and 1 fastball down the middle of the plate, I was already in attack mode and stroke the pitch to left center where Darryl and Devin McGinnis gave chase all the way to the fence some 350ft away.

"Go Cass, go," a Pirate yelled.

"Run lil' brother, run," Sonny said.

"All the way home," Carleone conjoled. "All the way home."

As I rounded second base and headed into third, I could see the centerfielder, Devin, had gotten to the ball quickly, but I was determined for my first homerun of the summer.

"Slide, slide," the on deck batter, Demarco, said. Demarco was the only person our age from the neighborhood who actually played organized ball, so I figured I had better get dirty. Funny, as I slid headfirst into home Mitch wasn't even trying to make an attempt to catch the ball and tag me out. A mouth full of dirt later, Demarco just looked down at me and said, "my bad Cassius, I thought they were coming home with it."

Sonny and Pops were closer than Pops and I, but everybody always said I could play ball just as good as Pops. The inside the park homer solidified that.

"That nigga ran them bases like his daddy," one spectator said. Another, Dope Fiend Dave, went one better. "Man, dat boy ran dem bases like E.T. McGee."

Marcus was mad enough to fight or at least throw a bean-ball at the next batter prompting a fight.

The Pirates were happy and I was confused.

"Who is E.T. McGee?" I asked Dope Fiend Dave as I spat the Terry Park dirt out of my mouth.

"Who is E.T. McGee?" Dave shot back. "You know kid, dat nigga dat play for the Cardinals."

"His name is Willie McGee," I corrected Dave in my youthful naiveté.

"We'll dat nigga uglier dan a motherfuckin' extraterrestrial," Dave protested. "Look jus like dat alien from the movie. 'E.T phone home. E.T. phone home'."

The whole park just erupted in laughter. Just when I thought it was about to get ugly with Marcus and his quick temper, the whole park just erupted in laughter.

CHAPTER 2:
LOVE AT FIRST SIGHT

We hadn't even finished completely moving in to our new digs, when I saw the prettiest girl ever in my young life. She was stunning. Strikingly stunning in her flower print summer dress and matching sunlit sandals, her hair fixed in curled pig tails and her skin was a caramel complexion. Tall for her age, she was probably an inch or so shorter than me, but she was still as fine as they come at eleven.

"My name is Gabriel, but my friends call me Gabby," she said, running up to me as I grabbed the last of my belongings off the makeshift moving truck Mom's younger brother Unc used to help us relocate. "What's your name?"

She was crass, and she was bold and somewhat rude, but I was smitten, excited by her presence.

"My name is Cassius," I countered, "but my friends call me Cass."

"Cassius what?" she asked.

"Whatta ya' mean?" I retorted.

"What's yo' full name?" she demanded.

"Oh," I said dumbfounded, "Cassius Clay Winston."

"How old are you Cassius Clay Winston," she demanded again.

"I'm eleven," I answered. "How old...?"

"I'm twelve and I'm oldest," she interrupted. "That means I run this."

"Run what," I asked.

"This."

"What's this?"

"Our relationship."

"What relationship?," I wanted to know.

"You my new boyfriend," she informed.

"Yo' what?"

"You heard me," she corrected, "my new boyfriend."

"How? Why? Whatta you saying?"

"I'm saying, I got first dibs on the new kid, so now you my boyfriend."

I was befuddled. Definitely shocked. I was about to continue to figure out Gabriel's angle when Moms pulled rank.

"Cassius!" Moms screamed out from the front door. "Quit messing with that fast tail lil' gal and get yo' butt over here."

Boy was I relieved. Moms had helped save me from a terrifying moment, but to tell the truth, it was more exciting than terrifying. I couldn't quite figure out Gabriel's motives. We hadn't even fully moved in our new home and I instantly became her boyfriend.

"I gotta go help my momma finish moving," I informed Gabriel. "I'on know when I'll see you again."

"Bye," she said, trying as hard as a twelve-year-old can to be sexy. "I'll see you later Cassius Clay Winston."

I didn't know the girl, but I was indeed mesmerized. As I helped the family finish sorting our things I couldn't help but wonder why Gabriel was all on me like that. I didn't mind, I just wondered. I did know I had to tell Sonny.

"Sonny," I said, when my big brother ventured back out to the front steps. "Do you believe in love at first sight?"

"Man, naw," Sonny barked, "why you ask?"

"I'on know," I chickened out, "I just asked."

CHAPTER 3:
HOT SUMMER NIGHTS

The first night in our new crib was cool. We had a central air and cooling unit that helped starve off the Midwest's August heat and humidity. Moms loved that. She crank the air up to a cool 65 degrees and marveled at the speed in which the entire three bedroom, three level townhouse was cooled. We even had cable TV.

Pops had called and told us his agent was told by the Cardinals that they were planning on calling Pops up to the big leagues when the rosters expanded on September 1.

More importantly though, Sonny and I had separate bedrooms. No longer did we have to share rooms and sleep on bunk beds. I could play with my army men in peace and he could talk to his girl-friends without my eavesdropping and picking up his Mack daddy lines.

Moms made my favorite that night, too; fried chicken, broccoli and cauliflower with Cheez-Wiz on top. Man, life was good.

"Now, ya'll listen," Moms said as Sonny and I set plates for dinner. "There are going to be some changes in how we live around here. It's time for you two to learn some responsibility. Sonny on Mondays, Wednesdays and Fridays you need to wash dishes."

"Moms..." Sonny protested to no avail.

"Boy, shut the hell up and listen," Moms said, rationing portion of fried chicken to her off-springs.

"Like I said, on Mondays, Wednesdays and Fridays you got dishes and Cass you take out the trash. On Tuesdays, Thursday and Saturdays, Cass, you wash dishes and Sonny you take out the trash. Ya'll rotate on Sundays. Tonight, Sonny is your night."

"Each night, I want my kitchen floor mopped. Take turns. Sonny, tonight's your night. Both of you are responsible for cleaning your own rooms and I want them done on Saturdays, along with the upstairs bathroom."

"Whatta ya' mean," Sonny interrupted again.

"I mean, Saturday, Sonny, you clean the bathroom and the Saturday after that, Cassius you clean it. Simple ain't it."

"And what you gon' do," Sonny foolishly asked.

"I'ma keep these damn lights and air on, put food on the table, clothed yo' ass, ya' know, things like that."

"You on pay no bills," Sonny smart mouthed. "Pops do."

"Yo' daddy don't pay a damn dime on no bills, boy," Moms corrected. "Shut the hell up and eat yo' damn food, Sonny, befoe I pop yo' ass right square in the mouth."

Sonny retreated, but I was surprised when Moms said Pops didn't pay any bills. I just knew he was chipping in on something. I was disheartened to find out other wise.

After dinner, Sonny and I started on our new chores. It was a late dinner, so by the time we were finished it was our bedtime. Moms had dosed off right after she eat dinner so by the time we were done cleaning the kitchen, she was sound asleep.

It was late and the only thing to do was stay up to watch television. Moms' master bedroom was on the lower level of the townhouse and our bedrooms were on the third floor, giving us more freedom than the law allowed.

After a brief home made session of Wrestling at the Chase, Sonny sent me to my room so he could whisper sweet nothings to one of his girlfriends from the Southside. I had no problem leaving, especially after Sonny put me in the full nelson and made me scream uncle.

"I'm telling Moms, watch," I cried out as Sonny relinquished his grip. "You gon' be in trouble."

"Shut up, fag," Sonny shot back. "You always talking 'bout telling Moms. Take yo' lil' punk ass to yo' room and you betta not say nothing or else it's on when she go to work in the morning."

Sonny was close to six feet tall at thirteen and sort of physical. He was way stronger than I, so the threat was well taken. I went straight to my room.

As I changed into sleep clothes, I kept hearing what sounded like a rock or pebble being pelted against my window. I was startled at first. I peeped through the window blinds and saw that cute girl Gabriel down below looking for more rocks to throw. The sight of her was comforting.

"Gabriel?" I asked, "whatta ya' doing?

"I'm trying to see my new boyfriend," she deadpanned. "Come on out."

"I can't" I retorted. "My momma'll kill me."

"Well, I'm coming up," she said.

I was stomped. "Coming up? Whatta ya' mean, coming up?"

"I'ma climb up there," she explained.

This girl is crazy, I thought. How in the world is she going to climb up my roof to get to my room? She easily showed me.

My room was in the back of the townhouse and right outside my bedroom window was the rooftop. Right below the rooftop was a ledge that connected the roof to our back porch. By jumping on the ledge, all Gabriel had to do was reach out and grab the roof and climb up. She did.

"Ain't 'chu gon' help me?" Gabriel barked as I watched in amazement.

"Sorry," I said sheepishly. I reached out to help her complete her mission.

Gabriel had changed from what she was wearing earlier, but that wasn't a bad thing. She wore khaki short pants and one of those yellow designer polo shirts from Lactose. The outfit fit her to a tee.

"Gabriel, what are you up to?" I asked as she tried to make her stint on my rooftop a comfortable one.

"Go get me a pillow, please Cassius," Gabriel demanded. "Cassius...ooohhh...I love that name. Cassius Clay Winston...ummm, you gon' be a star...my baby for life."

"Here you go," I offered, giving Gabriel the only pillow I had on my half bunk bed. "I like your name too. Well your first name at least. What's your whole name?"

"Gabriel Monique Robinson," she said, "my daddy named me."

"Where's your daddy at right now?" I wondered.

"Gone," she answered.

"Gone where?" I probed.

"Gone to meet his maker," she informed, sensing I was getting a little bit too nosey. "But I'on wanna talk about him right now, where yo' daddy?"

"My daddy is in Louisville," I boasted.

"Where's Louisville?" she unashamedly asked.

"In Kentucky," I answered, wondering "you ain't never heard of Louisville before?"

"No," she said matter of fact, "not ever. Why yo' daddy in Louisville? Don't he love ya'll."

"Yeah, girl, our daddy love us," I retorted. "He's down there playing baseball for the Cardinals."

"What'chu mean for the Cardinals?" Gabriel wondered. "I thought the Cardinals was from St. Louis."

"They are," I explained, "but they have a minor league team in Louisville and my daddy playing for them until the Cardinals call him up September 1."

"For real?" Gabriel said in amazement. "Yo' daddy play for the Cardinals?"

"Not yet, but almost," I cautioned.

I went on to break down to Gabriel how the minor league system works for major league baseball and when I was finished, she surprised me by giving me an innocent peck on the cheek.

"What was that for?" I asked.

"'Cause I like you," she answered, "and you my boyfriend."

She went on to explain to me how her mother had accidentally killed her father in self defense when Gabriel was five. She said family members had told her she was there when the incident happened, but she couldn't and wouldn't want to remember it happened. She said her father physically abused her and that is what she remembered

"A gang of ass whuppings," Gabriel called the abuse, "body slams and choke holds. I'm glad she shot him."

197

"Where's your momma?" I asked.

"At work." Gabriel answered. "She leaves at ten at night and comes home at eight in the morning, screaming at me and my lil' sister about what kinda work we ain't done the night before, while my big brother get to do whatever he wanna do. Where yo' momma?"

"Hopefully in her room sleep," I answered, "she goes to work in the morning time."

"Well that's cool," Gabriel assured, "I'ma gon' go in the house befoe my Grandmomma wake up and be wondering where I'm at. You wanna help me down?"

As Gabriel made her way off of the rooftop and onto the back porch, I heard the sound of car window being smashed. I looked out toward the alley and by the time I looked back at Gabriel she had booked. Before long the car alarm was blazing and I didn't know what to do. I didn't know whose car it was, so I decided to just close my window and mind my business.

One of the three car thieves looked right at me as I closed my blinds, but I prayed he didn't see me. I'd seen him, so he must had seen me. I thought about informing Sonny, but remembered the all out assault I had just received from him and scrapped that idea.

I decided to go to sleep and not even worry about the car thieves. I didn't know them and they didn't know me. Besides I wanted to hurry up and get to bed so that I could dream about Gabriel's pretty self.

CHAPTER 4:
A BRAND NEW DAY

Man, was I happy when I woke up the morning after our first night on James Cool. Moms had already left for work. Usually it was Romper Room around the house when she left for work. No sooner did I come from my room to engage Sonny in a rematch from the night before that I heard the most annoying ear piercing screech.

"Eh, eh, eh," the screech bellowed. "Eh, eh, eh." It was a female's screech and it was coming from Sonny's room. I had to find out what was going on.

"Sonny!" I yelled as I jiggled the locked doorknob of Sonny's room. "What's going on in there?"

After a brief moment of tussling and a few 'baby, be quiets', Sonny came to his door, unlocked it, cracked it and politely told me to "burnout, you lil' motherfucka, go outside and play some catch or something."

"I ain't got no body to play catch with," I replied, trying to sneak-a-peek at one of Sonny's girlfriends.

"Play with yo' self, for all I care," Sonny suggested, "just get the hell outta here."

I was distraught. There we were in a brand new townhouse, I had no friends and my brother wouldn't play catch with me because he was banging some chick. "I'ma tell Moms," I warned, "and she gon' beat yo' butt."

"And I'ma beat yo' ass," Sonny said soon before the screeching began again. "Now scram, twerp."

I bugged out for a minute before I realized why I woke up happy in the first place. I had me a girlfriend and she was pretty brown sugar, baby. I grabbed my glove and baseball and made a mad dash for Gabriel's house.

"Who is it?" a grumpy sounded older female voice said from behind Gabriel's family door. "Who do you want?" the voice said after I introduced myself.

"Is Gabriel there?" I asked through the door.

"Yeah, she here, but she can't have no boy company, young man."

"Huh?"

"I said, she ain't allowed no boy company. So, go on away from here and wake up somebody else."

I was saddened. The older lady had hurt my feelings. "How am I suppose to know she can't have no company?" I screamed before kicking the door and high-tailing it on back to our place.

Much to my delight, when I got back around to our place I realized Moms had left two pancake and cheesy egg platters for Sonny and I. I smashed mines and I guess the adrenaline rush of being chased away from Gabriel's had me thinking unclearly because I smashed Sonny's platter as well.

Only after I finished the last syrup drenched pancake did I remember what happened to me the last time I ate one of Sonny's meal.

I picked up the telephone and called my grandma. I would have called Moms, but she always told us to call Granny if we had a problem while she was at work. I called Granny often.

"Hello, Granny?" I said when my grandma answered the phone.

"Yeah, baby?"

"Granny, Sonny gon' get me."

"Why? What did you do to Sonny?"

"Nothing."

"Nothing? Now, come on baby, Granny know you done did something to make Sonny wanna get you."

"I mean, I ate his breakfast."

"Oh, baby, you know you ain't suppose to eat nobody's food but your own. Now, you know I'on condone siblings fighting, but if Sonny taxes yo' backside then you deserve it today. Where Sonny at? Put him on the phone."

"I can't. He in his room with some girl."

"What? What some girl?

"I'on know. Some girl."

"Boy, you done done it now. You kids. I done told Virginia ya'll don't need to be there watching ya'll self. I'm on my way ova there."

I knew Sonny was going to be mad at me, but he had made me mad by putting me out of the house. Then that older lady didn't make it any better. I shouldn't have eaten Sonny's breakfast. I made my way back upstairs.

"Sonny," I cautioned, "Granny said she on her way over here."

"What?"

"You heard me. You betta get that girl outta here."

"You snitched on me twerp?" Sonny said after quickly escorting the girl out of the backdoor.

"Nigga, you know Pam came way over here from the Southside to spend the day with me. Skipped Operation Brightside and everything to come see me and you gon' snitch."

I broke to the bathroom and locked the door.

"Come outta there Cass and get this ass whupping," Sonny threatened. "Come on out. Granny ain't finna save you from this ass whupping, boy."

After a brief silence, I thought I was safe. I was going to come out of the bathroom, but I remembered Sonny had pulled that trick on me before. I decided to stay put until Granny got there.

"Bring yo' lil' ass on outta there," Sonny screamed after another moment of silence. He was now trying to break the bathroom door down. "I'ma beat yo' ass, boy."

It was close to noon when Granny finally arrived and I was relieved. In those couple of hours in the bathroom I got a chance to take a bath, brush my teeth six times and try on some of Sonny's deodorant and cologne. I even took Sonny's clippers to my head, putting a part on the left side of my head, right above the temple. It was kind of crooked, but I liked it. It was my first part and I thought I looked cool like Sonny looked whenever he put a part in his hair. I even took a nap.

"Come on outta that bathroom, baby," Granny said. "Come on nye. Granny tired and need to use that bathroom."

"Hey, Granny," I said, smiling as I opened the bathroom door. "How you.." Before I could finish, my grandma reached out and grabbed my collar.

"What have I told you 'bout lying on your brother?" she screamed. "Now, I'ma beat yo' ass." And with that, I took one of those classic grandmotherly beat-downs, complete with the 'gon and get something to wipe yo' face off' pep talk.

After the belt whipping, I retreated to my room and took refuge by climbing onto the rooftop outside my window. I wanted to daydream about Gabriel and the kiss on the cheek she'd given me.

It's one thing to sit on the roof late at night and a whole different subject in the middle of the day.

The St. Louis heat is unforgiving on those late summer days and that day was no exception. No more than ten minutes on the roof, I realized I needed my favorite summer past-time; sunflower seeds and lemonade.

Pops had put me on to the concoction during one of his stories about traveling and playing in the minor leagues. "That's the key to get to the bigs, Cass," Pops would say. "You gotta enjoy every minute of it." I'd been hooked since nine.

The most pleasant of surprises greeted me when I returned to the rooftop. Two guys, probably around Sonny's age, were in the backyard getting set to play a game of cork ball. They each had a glove, two tennis balls and a cork bat. We'd played plenty of cork-ball over on Park Ave., but we preferred the League ball. We also had plenty of open space with Terry Park and the vacant lot at the beginning of the 3400 block of Park Ave.

Over on James Cool, all the vacant lots had been redeveloped into town-homes and Chambers Park was too close to the Bluemeyer Housing Projects for JVL tenants to play ball in.

Watching the two guys warm up, it was obvious they were brothers. I didn't know if they noticed me on the rooftop, but after a few seeds and a glass of Moms' finest, sweetest lemonade, I got an idea.

"How 'bout a game of three-man?" I yelled as the brothers' attention turned upward toward the rooftop.

They glanced at each other, smiled, and the older, taller one asked, "who is you?"

"My name Cassius," I answered. "Me and my brother Sonny just moved in the neighborhood."

"Aw yeah," the younger one said to his brother, "daddy 'nem said someone just moved on the side of us."

The configuration of our townhouse was a three-plex. It was our place, 2931 James Cool Papa Bell. Right next door at 2931 1/2 was Marlin and Cynthia's place and on the side of us were the two brothers and their family's place, 2929. Right across from them was Gabriel's family's place at 2927. Gabriel's family place and the brothers' place formed a gangway that led to the backyard and front. Gabriel's family's place was part of another three-plex.

"Can you hit?" the younger one continued.

"Sure," I said modestly, "I can hit."

"Well, come down and show us what you got."

I grabbed my glove for the second time that day, but I left the league ball in the house. I told Granny, who had stayed over after my beating to look after us, that I was going out back to play ball and was stopped dead in my tracks.

"Are you asking me or telling me?" Granny cajoled. "'Cause if you asking me, it sure don't sound like it."

"Granny can I please go out back and play cork ball, please?"

"Now, that's more like it," she gushed, preaching to me about the sanctity of not lying on my brother.

"But, I didn't lie on him Granny, he did have some girl over here this morning."

"Well, Sonny said you lied on him 'cause he was going to beat you for eating his breakfast."

"That ain't even true, Granny. He didn't even know nothing about no breakfast."

"Hush, now boy, and go outside and play. Everybody know how you like to play make believe.

Now get on outta here. Bye."

CHAPTER 5:
NEW FOUND FRIEND

The younger brother, Greg, was a cool dude. The older one, Gerald, was intimidating like Marcus McGinnis over on the Southside. Greg and I talked baseball for hours. Not only did he like baseball, he was a Cardinals fan like me. He had even heard of Pops.

"Pops Winston yo' daddy?" he asked upon the discovery. "Man, that's messed up. Vince got left field locked down. Willie ain't going nowhere. And the white boy, Van Slyke? Aw, he cold, dog. You know he ain't going nowhere?"

"I know, but he is supposed to be getting a September call up."

"For real? Man, that'll be cool."

Greg asked me a few more questions about Pops and then we started talking about the big league club, which was in the middle of a pennant race with the hated pond scum Mets and dreaded Cubs.

"So you telling me that Willie McGee is better than Ozzie," I said when Greg made the comparison.

"Man, Willie got the speed, the power, he can hit for average, catch anything in sight and he be throwing cats out at the plate," he explained.

"But, Ozzie is...Ozzie," I argued.

"Besides back-flips and diving catches," Greg argued, "what else can he do? No homers. He can't hit and they say his shoulder is messed up."

"Dude, you crazy. Ozzie is way colder than E.T. McGee."

Greg had made a convincing argument about Willie McGee being a better player than Ozzie Smith, but I wasn't buying it. Ozzie was just...Ozzie.

"Why you call him E.T. McGee," Greg asked about the line I'd stolen from Dope Fiend Dave.

"'Cause that nigga's uglier than an extraterrestrial. 'E.T. phone home. E.T. phone home.'"

"Cassius, you'sa fool," Greg snickered. "You'sa crazy fool. That is funny as shit. E.T. McGee."

Our conversation had carried us to the front stoop of our townhouse porch. I'd put Greg up on the sunflower seed and lemonade concoction and we continued to talk Cardinal baseball. Out of nowhere, Greg thought of an excellent idea to prove who was a better player, Ozzie or Willie.

"Let's go to the game tonight," Greg offered.

"What'chu mean?"

"I mean, lets go to the game tonight and find out whose better."

"How we gon' do that?"

I've been cutting grass all summer saving up to go school shopping, but I got enough saved for a couple of Cardinal tickets."

"For real, dawg?"

"Yeah. All you gotta do is make sure you get yo' daddy to sign me a ball when he make it to the Big Leagues."

"That's it?"

"Yep, that's it."

"Aw man, that's cool. Look, my momma gets home at about three thirty, four o'clock. As soon as she get here I'll asked her."

"Where she at? Work?"

"Yep."

"Where yo' momma work at?"

"I'on know, some nursing home on the Southside."

"Oh, yeah? That's where ya'll from? The Southside?"

"Yeah. Why you say it like that? The Southside."

"It's cool, I just hope the JVL posse don't find that out, 'cause they sho' be tripping with fools from the Southside."

"Aw, man I ain't worried about that. Ain't nobody gon' mess with us. My brother Sonny, he crazy and he can fight."

"That's cool, Cassius, just remember what I tell you. Them JVL Posses cats don't like Southside niggas, so don't tell'em ya'll from the Southside."

"Anyway, man, when we leaving for the game?"

"Let's leave here about five, so we can get down there and watch batting practice."

"How we gon' get there? My momma don't have no car."

"For real? How she get to work everyday then?"

"I'on know, some man named Fast Freddy be taking her and dropping her off."

"That's cool. We gonna walk anyway."

"Walk? All the way downtown to Busch Stadium?"

"Yeah."

"And you said I was crazy. Nigga you crazy. I ain't walking in this heat. Besides, my momma ain't going for that."

"My parents ain't going for that either, so we gonna tell time we getting on the Bi-State. The *32 Martin Luther King* will take us straight downtown. We just gonna walk the bus line way."

"Aw'ight," I concurred. "So, I'll knock on yo' door once my momma gets back."

"Cool. Jus' don't forget to tell yo' daddy he gotta sign me a ball when he get his call up."

Sonny and Granny had conspired together so that Sonny could go with her once Moms got home from work, so my chances of Moms saying yes to the baseball game had increased.

That Fast Freddy dude had been hanging around a lot before we moved, so I figured he would be hanging around on James Cool too. Moms insisted he was just a friend and grown folks could have friends of the opposite sex and it still be a friendship. I hoped that all it was was a friendship because Pops would be home in September and he probably wouldn't like Freddy being around all the time.

My argument was Moms could kick it with Freddy with the kids gone for the evening and surprisingly she bit.

"So who is this Craig guy, and where does he live?" Moms demanded.

"His name is Greg, Moms, Greg and he lives on the side of us."

"Craig, Greg. Same thing. Who is his momma?"

"I'on know."

"Well, damn who is the daddy?"

"I'on know Moms. I just know they live on the side of us."

After the brief exchange of wits, Moms decided to go meet our new neighbors on the side; Tony and Angie Jones, father of April, Gerald, Greg, June Bug and Marvin.

"Nice to meet you all," Moms charmed, "and Greg you and Cass here, ya'll betta call Tony as soon as that game is over, you hear?"

"Yes ma'am," Greg and I said in unison."

Greg and I were amped. We had our gloves. We had our red STL Cardinals baseball hats with the birds on the bat and we had our sunflower seeds.

"We gonna get lemonade at the stadium," Greg insisted. "I'on wanna drink up all of yo' momma's stuff."

At five o'clock that evening Greg and I were ready to make our move. We were going to catch the *32 MLK* down to Busch and have Tony pick us up. At least, that's what Moms and Greg's parents thought. We were sticking to our plans of walking downtown and the baseball Gods must have known that we were up to no good.

That hot and hazy August day had turned into a humid and dry evening. The scorching sun had mysteriously vanished behind a few overcastted clouds. Just as we were about to start our trek to the game, the rain came. We were young boys, so we didn't care about umbrellas, clouds or rains. They knew baseball was never played in that weather, so Moms and the Jones' pulled rank.

"Tomorrow will be nice and sunny," Moms chimed. "Ya'll can go tomorrow."

Just great. Sonny was gone for the weekend. The Cardinals' game was rained out. And that Fast Freddy guy was spending the evening with Moms. I was very disappointed, so I did what most eleven year olds would do. I stirred trouble.

"Moms. I wanna talk to Pops," I started.

"What, boy?" Moms answered from the depths of the bottom floor.

"I wanna talk to Pops," I screamed again.

"Boy, yo' daddy's got a game tonight in Louisville somewhere. You can't talk to him. Watch some t.v or something before I come up them steps and tear something up."

"I on wanna watch no t.v," I snapped before realizing I had already taken a beating from Granny earlier in the day. "I'm hungry."

"I know, baby," Moms flipped. "Give momma a minute. I'ma put some fish and spaghetti on the stove for you."

"For real?"

"Yeah, baby, just give me a minute."

Moms knew after broccoli and cauliflower with cheese and fried chicken, spaghetti and fish was my second favorite dish. Moms knew that would quiet me down.

The excitement of the day had caught up with me that evening and I dosed off. I had a portable radio. A Sony Walkman to be exact. I usually listened to Cardinals' games on KMOX with it, but when Jack Buck and Mike Shannon announced a rain out, I decided to listen to Majic 108-FM and they were actually playing some nice tunes. In fact, I woke up from dosing off thinking I was in the middle of a mid-80's music video. I removed the headphones from my ears and looked out of my back window and there she was. Gabriel, looking better than the day before, was sitting on my rooftop.

"Gabriel, what are you doing?" I asked sheepishly.

"Waiting on you to come out here and keep me company."

"When did it stop raining?"

"About an hour ago."

"Man, I was suppose to go to the Cardinals' game with Greg."

"Who?"

"Greg. He stays next door to ya'll."

"Oh. I know who you talking about."

"Why didn't ya'll go?"

"It started raining. We going tomorrow, though."

"I wanna go."

"You can't go."

"Why?"

"Because you a girl and girls don't know nothing about no baseball."

208

"I'on care nothing about no baseball, I just wanna hang out with you."

"We hanging now."

"Whatever. Anyway, I'm hungry. What yo' momma cook?"

I had forgotten all about dinner. How could I forget about the Friday night special?

"Fish and spaghetti. My momma cooked fish and spaghetti."

"Ooowwwweee, I want some. Go fetch me a plate."

"For real?"

"Yeah, boy, I'm hungry."

"I'ma ask my momma."

"You ain't gotta do all that. Just go sneak me a plate or give me some of yours."

"I can't give you some of mines."

"Why not?"

"Because I gotta eat at the kitchen table."

"That's why I said go sneak me a plate. She don't have to know."

I was enamored with Gabriel. I would run through a brick wall for her, but to subject myself to another belt whipping wasn't happening that day.

"I can't. I'ma get a whupping."

"Don't you love me? Ain't I yo' girlfriend?"

"Uh, yeah."

"Well, go sneak me a plate."

I made my way through my room, down the stairs and into the kitchen. Before I could actually make it into the kitchen, I heard yelling and screaming coming from Moms room on the basement level. I couldn't help but hear her and that Fast Freddy guy arguing.

"Look Freddy, I done told you I ain't getting no damn abortion. I'm keeping this baby."

"What about yo' husband, GiGi? Homeboy ain't gone like that shit."

"My husband ain't got nothing to do with the fact you laid yo' seed in me. Besides, I done told you me and Rob getting a divorce as soon as he gets back in town."

"I'll believe it when I see it."

"Wait, where the hell you going? You just gone walk out on me like that."

"I told you how I feel about having a baby with a married women, GiGi. Now respect that."

"Fool, you what'n saying that when we was laying up screwing, now was you. Now, I'm all tied up and now you wanna bounce. Then bounce nigga. I'on need you or Robert or no nigga for that matter. I can raise my kids by my damn self."

I really didn't know what to make of the argument, but I knew I had to get back to Gabriel with her plate before Moms caught me. By the time I'd fixed the plate and headed back to the rooftop, Fast Freddy had left and Gabriel was missing in action.

"Boo! Gotcha!" Gabriel screamed from behind my closet door, making the plate and a little pee hit the floor.

"Cassius?" Moms screamed out, "what was that noise?"

"Nothing, Moms," I assured, leaning over the third floor hallway banister. "I dropped my league ball."

"Quit making all that noise and come down here and fix you a plate of something to eat."

"Could you make it for me Moms," I said as I escorted Gabriel back out onto the rooftop. "I gotta finish making my bed."

"Make it fast, now baby, momma is tired."

"O.K."

"Cassius Clay Winston, you are so sweet," Gabriel said, before climbing down off the rooftop. "Lying to yo' momma and sneaking me a plate. Come here, I wanna give you a kiss."

She kissed me again. That time real soft and real quick on the lips. "I'll see you later," she said before disappearing into an unusually cool St. Louis summer night. She promised she'd come back after her mother left for work so that we could watch Friday Night Videos on Channel 5 together. Moms would kill me if she knew what Gabriel and I had planned.

The plan never materialized. Shortly after devouring my plate of fish and spaghetti at the kitchen table Moms sent me back upstairs so she could clean the kitchen. It was my night to clean, but I wasn't going to argue, so I did as I was told.

"Thank you, Moms," I said, sensing she was feeling a little down. "Food was good. I love you."

"Aww, baby momma love you too," she countered. "Come give yo' momma a kiss."

The moment of truth. I still had Gabriel's lip smack still on my brain and I didn't want to spoil it by kissing Moms on the lips. Problem was, I always kissed Moms on the lips. Always.

"Ohhh," Moms complained, "you done found you a lil' something hot in the neighborhood and now you'ont wanna kiss yo' momma. Boy, these lil' nappy headed girls can't never take the place of yo' momma's love and affection. Now, bring yo' lil' butt here and lay it on me. C'mon now."

"Good night, Moms, love you again," I said after Moms planted a wet one on me.

"Yeah, I know you do," she smart mouthed, "Now, go 'head upstairs so I can clean this kitchen.

I woke up awhile later to the fuzziness of late night television, checked the rooftop and went back to sleep. I figured Gabriel probably had eaten, got lazy and feel asleep just like I did. On the other hand, maybe she was waiting on the perfect time to come back.

I had a choice. Post up on the rooftop for a while or go back to sleep. I reasoned since I had just had a nap a few hours earlier I would stay up and wait awhile for Gabriel. I grabbed my walkman and headed to the rooftop. Gabriel never showed. I wasn't mad though. It was late and she was probably sleeping. I didn't go back inside until the sun came up, but to see the sun rise at that age was a fascinating thing.

"Damn," was all I could muster as the burnt orange sun rose that early morning.

CHAPTER 6:
FIELD OF DREAMS

"Yo, Cass," a voice yelled out, "what'chu doing sleep on the roof, dog?"

It was Greg hanging out of his room's window that was exactly next to my rooftop, although the rooftop didn't extend far enough for him to reach it from his window.

I guess he was surprised to see me on the roof that early in the morning. It was close to nine and I had passed out on the rooftop after staying awake to watch the sun rise. I was actually waiting on Gabriel, but in her absence, the reddish-orange fire of the sun became my company.

"Man, I was watching the sun rise this morning," I explained, "and it was the coolest thing I ever seen in my life."

"Word?" Greg pondered, "you stayed up all night to watch the sun come up?"

"Well, not all night," I explained, "I woke up around three o' clock in the morning and came out here to watch it."

"Lil' dude, you weird as hell," the older brother Gerald interrupted. "I ain't never heard of nobody staying up all night to watch no sun come up."

"I ain't weird, I just like hanging out on rooftops, watching the sun rise," I protested. "What do you like to do?"

"I like chasing skirts, lil' nigga," Gerald badgered, "where yo' big sista at?"

"I ain't got no sisters," I corrected.

"Well, lil' nigga, we ain't got nothing to talk about," Gerald said, pulling back from the window. He teased Greg.

"That lil' nigga weird, man."

"Man, leave my partna alone," Greg stepped up, "he cool. Yo Cass, what time we leaving for the game? You know it starts at 12:05 today, right?"

"For real?" I asked in amazement, "I thought it was a 1:15 game."

"Naw, that's tomorrow," Greg assured, "they playing at noon today. I think it's the Game of the Week on Channel 5 or something."

"Man, I'ma go wash up and get ready then," I said. "We got to get down there early, so we can watch batting practice."

"Aw'ight," Greg said, "make it fast, 'cause I'm already ready to go."

The rain from the night before had made it sort of a dreary day, but the thunderstorms were just passing through. The news said it was supposed to be sunny all that day, but it was cloudy instead. Moms was using that as an excuse not to give me the money she said she was going to give me the night before.

"Boy, it's gon' rain," she argued, "ya'll don't need to be going to no baseball game."

"The newsman said it was going to be sunny all day, though, Moms," I countered.

"Look outside, boy," she continued, "where the sun at."

"It' ain't gon' rain, Moms," I promised half-hearted. "Besides, it's the Mets' game. We gotta go."

"Boy here," Moms gave in, "take this five dollars and don't spend it all in one place."

Greg's parents, Tony and Angie took us down to Busch Stadium that afternoon, but we had missed batting practice. We still had our gloves and red Cardinals ballcaps, so we decided we were going to somehow come up with a ball anyway. Tony and Angie gave us specific instructions to call them as soon as the game was over, but Greg had a plan.

"Daddy, we walking home after game," he said to Tony, nudging me for back up.

"Yeah, Mr. Tony," I offered, "we walking home after the game."

Tony was unmoved. "Ya'll call as soon as the game is over and we'll be back down here to pick ya'll up," he barked. "Later."

213

The game was intense. The Mets had a bunch of superstar bad boys on their team; Daryl Strawberry, Gary Carter, El Sid, Ron Darling, Doc Gooden and the most hated, former Cardinal Keith Hernandez. Cardinal Nation got a kick out of teasing Daryl Strawberry, though. Whenever Strawberry went to his post in right field, the right field bleacher section would yell out, "Darrrryl. Darrrryl. Darrrryl."

It was the funniest thing in the world to us, so we joined in the chorus. "Darrrryl. Darrrrryl. Darrrrryl," we bellowed in unison with the other bleacher creatures, "Darrrryl."

We repeated the trick for seven innings that afternoon and the only thing that shut us up was Strawberry's monster blast of a home-run into the same cheap seats that teased him. Trotting back to his position toward the bottom of the seventh, the bleachers were quiet and Strawberry ate it up.

"I can't hear you," Strawberry screamed to no one in particular. Holding his ear for emphasis, he taunted some more. "Why ya'll ain't saying nothing?"

After taking warm up tosses from his centerfielder, Strawberry turned toward the bleachers again.

He pumped fake throwing the ball into the stands, only to re-cock and let it hang. He hurled the ball into the bleacher seats and the whole section made their move. I was amped. I just knew the ball was coming to me. I hit a couple of steps, moved around an older couple sitting in the bleachers and bo-guarded around a youngster my age and made the catch. A hefty applause sounded throughout the bleacher section and the chant started again. Instead of a heckling chant, it was more of a cheering chant.

"Dar'ryl, Dar'ryl, Dar'ryl!" the bleachers erupted. "Dar'ryl, Dar'ryl." Strawberry tipped his hat and got prepared for the first pitch of the inning. Meanwhile, Greg was impressed.

"Damn," Greg said, "you got a ball from Darryl Strawberry. Dog, we gotta get his autograph after the game. We got to."

After receiving pats on the back from fellow bleacher creatures, I took my newfound famous self to the concession stand. I wanted a hot dog and soda, but Greg recommended nachos.

"You ain't never had Busch Stadium nachos?" Greg asked. "You'nt know what you missing."

Unfortunately, the Cardinals lost that afternoon. Too much Darryl Strawberry, I guess, but Greg and I still had the plan of getting his autograph. We politicked with the ushers for about an hour after the game until one of them relented and took my new ball into the visitors' clubhouse for the Straw Man to sign. A few minutes later the usher reappeared with the signed ball. It read: "Good Luck, Darryl Strawberry, The Straw Man."

"Thank you, thank you," I said to the usher in all my youthful enthusiasm, "thank you."

CHAPTER 7:
THE JVL POSSE

Like typical adolescent youth, Greg and I defied all orders and walked our way home after the Mets' game. Tony, Angie and Moms were all going to be mad, but we took a chance anyway.

"Dog, I still can't believe you got a ball from Darryl Strawberry," Greg reiterated. "Now you got two League balls."

"I know, huh?" I responded. "Wait until I tell Pops. I'ma be like 'Pops, guess who threw me a ball and I caught it all the way up in the bleachers. He gon' be like 'Who?' I'ma be like 'Darryl Strawberry.' Eww, he might get mad though."

"Why that?" Greg wondered.

"Man, he just like us."

"WE HATE THE METS," Greg and I screamed in unison, starting a homerun style trot up toward Market Street. "WE HATE POND SCUM!"

Once we hit Market Street, we headed west on Market to Tucker, jaywalking and dodging traffic all the same. We continued jogging north on Tucker, slowing to a walk only after hitting Delmar Avenue and Tucker.

"You wanna stop at this gas station, Cass?" Greg suggested.

"For what?" I snipped. "I'on got no more money."

"Me neither," Greg joked. "Busch Stadium got all my bread today."

As we continued to walk east on Delmar, Greg got real serious with me.

"Hey, man, what school you going to next year?"

"I'on know, why you ask?"

"You'nt know?"

"I mean, Moms don't know if she gon' send us to Columbia Middle or a county school."

"What county school?"

"I'on know, she ain't filled out the papers yet."

"What she waitin' on?"

"I'on know, I guess to get settled in. Why you ask?"

"Just wondering."

"Why you wondering? What school you going to?"

"Parkway Central Junior High."

"For real?"

"Yep. I'ma be in the eighth grade. My brother Gerald gonna be a freshman at the senior high and

April's a sophomore. June Bug and Marvin go to the elementary school."

"Dang, ya'll whole family go to a county school, huh?"

"Yep. We started last year."

Greg went on to break the school desegregation program down to me. He explained how parents had three choices of suburban St. Louis school districts to voluntarily send their inner-city school aged children. Suburban school districts had more money, Greg said, and better books and better lunches. He even said they had computers.

"And the white girls are starting to like dudes from the city," Greg informed. "Something about that whole 'woe is the black man's plight' shit they be hearing about on the news. It's cool with me though, 'cause they be buying my lunch and giving me gifts on holidays. Birthdays, Christmases, Valentine's Day. Man, they even get me something on *they* birthday, fool. I'm talking 'bout some nice gifts too, dog."

I was intrigued. I couldn't wait to get home and tell Moms about my new baseball and Parkway Central.

"Man, I wanna go to ya'll school," I said enthusiastically. "It sounds better than going to Columbia."

"Ya'll betta hurry up. Tell yo' momma to hurry up and sign them papers 'cause everybody and they momma trying to get up in Parkway."

As we continued east on Delmar, passing Jefferson Boulevard and then Leffingwell Avenue in the process, Greg continue to talk about his experiences in The County.

"You know who house this is?" Greg asked, pointing to a home on Delmar that looked more like a tourist attraction than a living quarter.

"Nope," I surrendered. "Whose"

"That's the Scott Joplin House, man" Greg chided. "These damn city schools don't teach niggas shit for real, do they?"

R.I.P. Nose
Gone, but never forgotten.
You are loved and missed by many.

ABOUT THE AUTHOR:

From the depths of Park Avenue in South Saint Louis, Missouri emerges Toriano Porter, one of the quintessential literary voices of the 21st century.

The Pride of Park Avenue is Porter's first published book. He is a former All-Conference football player at both Eureka High School in Eureka, Missouri and Central Missouri State University in Warrensburg and a former minor league football All-America for the St. Louis Bulldogs. A news reporter with the Examiner newspaper in Independence, Missouri, his work has also appeared in publications such as the St. Louis American, St. Louis Evening Whirl, St. Louis Post-Dispatch, Riverfront Times, The Pitch, inBox Magazine, Playback STL Magazine, Central News Magazine, ENVY Magazine in Kansas City, www.stlhiphop.com and the Houston Press.

T.E.A.M. NiTRO PRESENTS....
Toriano Porter
The Pride of Park Avenue
featuring Rory L. Watkins
Copyright 2008

Author Contact Information
Toriano Porter
T.E.A.M. NiTRO
P.O. Box 32003
St. Louis, MO 63132
torianoporter@gmail.com
www.myspace.com/prideofparkavenue

images and photos courtesy of Amy Elrod
www.amyelrod.com
editor, Amy Brown Gander, T.E.A.M. NiTRO
www.myspace.com/niteowlsteam

49877300R00146

Made in the USA
San Bernardino, CA
26 August 2019